THE BOARD GAME FAMILY

RECLAIM YOUR CHILDREN FROM THE SCREEN

ELLIE DIX

Crown House Publishing Limited
www.crownhouse.co.uk

First published by
Crown House Publishing
Crown Buildings, Bancyfelin, Carmarthen, Wales, SA33 5ND, UK
www.crownhouse.co.uk

and

Crown House Publishing Company LLC
PO Box 2223, Williston, VT 05495, USA
www.crownhousepublishing.com

British Library of Cataloguing-in-Publication Data
A catalogue entry for this book is available from the British Library.

Print ISBN 978-178583433-2
Mobi ISBN 978-178583444-8
ePub ISBN 978-178583445-5
ePDF ISBN 978-178583446-2

LCCN 2015930350

Printed and bound in the UK by
Gomer Press, Llandysul, Ceredigion

For my own board game family.

CONTENTS

WHY YOU NEED BOARD GAMES AS PART OF YOUR FAMILY LIFE

THE PURPOSE OF THIS BOOK

This book is aimed at parents who want to spend more time with their children, and enjoy it. When you have older children in the house, it is not unusual to go through an entire week or more without having a proper conversation with them. Indeed, most conversations with young adults are transactional: arranging lifts, lending money, negotiating meals … For many parents, the in-depth debriefs about the school day, the anxious heart-to-hearts about worries and the excited outpourings of triumphs and successes disappeared around the child's tenth birthday (if they ever did happen). Although it may be normal to barely speak to your children, that doesn't mean it is right for us as parents or for them. However, it isn't easy to just strike up a proper conversation with someone who is permanently shielded by headphones and giving off 'leave me alone' signals. For conversation to flow naturally, we need to spend good chunks of time face-to-face with our children. You can't have a proper conversation through a door.

It can be challenging to share time with your children, particularly if they've reached that awkward stage at which they appear to be doing what they can to avoid you. The amount of time I want to spend with my own children can depend on what mood they are in, how many jobs I have to do and whether I'm equipped with a nice cold glass of my favourite tipple. But even when life is busy and tensions are high, I yearn for some quality time with them. I expect you do too; that is why you are here.

This book will help you to reconnect with your children through introducing board games to the family home. I understand that the idea of your kids willingly skipping downstairs when the 'family bell' sounds on a Sunday afternoon, calling excitedly for their younger siblings and declaring that they'd just *love* to embark on a three-hour epic game with the whole family may have you snorting tea out of your nose. So let me make a few points about the realities of family gaming:

- I do not live in the Little House on the Prairie and I know you don't either.
- You do not have to play long games, ever. Unless you want to. There are loads of brilliant games that fit happily into a 20-minute slot.
- You don't have to play games as a whole family. Nobody should ever be forced into playing.
- You don't need to set a pre-scheduled time for playing.
- Family games are so much more than they used to be, so abandon your preconceptions. The choice and quality available will blow your mind (and your children's).
- If you follow the ideas in this book, game playing will become normalised in your family. At some point your children will bolt downstairs to play and you'll not even raise an eyebrow, let alone splutter out your tea.

Through reading this book, you'll find out how to hook your children into board gaming through clever exposure and stealth tactics. You'll discover your own love of playing games and, in the process, develop your skills as a player and as a teacher of board games. You'll learn how to navigate through the choppy seas of sibling rivalry, minimising the arguments and the tears, and promoting gamesmanship. You'll modify and redesign those games you already own to better suit the family. You'll discover your sweet spots, finding games that work well for you and your children that don't break the bank. And, crucially, you'll become a master of the metagame: the most important game of all.

This is *not* an encyclopaedia of games. Although I will mention lots of different games and point you in the direction of ones that your family might enjoy, this book is not designed as a reference guide to every game you may ever want to play. There are thousands of new games released every year, and I won't even play 1 per cent of them (and I play a *lot* of games). There are already some outstanding resources available for you to conduct your own research, so I'll point you in the right direction and show you where to look.

When I mention a game in the book, it will be to illustrate a point. Don't expect full explanations of rules or detailed reviews because you won't get them here. Any game which is set in **bold italics** is listed in the appendix, where each entry includes a brief overview of the game and key information about game length, player count, etc. To find out more about these games, you can search for video and blog reviews online, where you'll find play-throughs, reviews and explanations of the rules. The appendix is designed to be an aid to the discussion in this book, rather than a go-to reference for all things board game related.

WHY ME?

Someone recently asked me what skills board games have taught me. For me, that question is a bit like asking what skills you've developed due to having a sister, or from going to school. It is a big question and practically impossible to answer. Board games have been woven through the very fabric of my life, so I can't disconnect that one element to make a judgement about their impact on me. Games have just always been there as a completely normal activity. I know that playing games has contributed enormously to my ability to interact with others, manage failure, work creatively with available resources, experiment with multiple paths to success, solve interesting problems, adapt to changing situations and make decisions quickly. But I don't have another non-board-gaming version of me to compare myself with, so I can't know what I would have been like without games. Nor do I really want to.

I love board games. I loved them when I was a child and I still love them now. I love that each game provides a potted experience in a box. Whether I'm a farmer making decisions about field planning and crop rotation, one of a group of people running from an erupting volcano or a space explorer trying to expand my own civilisation, I'm able to immerse myself in the world of the game and the puzzles and problems presented by the mechanics. I get absorbed in the decision-making process, trying to optimise the outcomes as best I can. There is real pleasure to be found in making discoveries and testing out new strategies.

When I was a child, all my friends' families had board games at home and played them regularly. Being a board game family was unremarkable. In my case, however, a few other ingredients were thrown into the mix that may have cemented my fate as a lifelong game lover. My mum was a senior lecturer in primary mathematics at Homerton College, Cambridge. She loved teaching maths through games and would often make up her own and test them out on my sister and me, before trying them with her students. Mum is a great believer in the importance of mastery of mental mathematics and believes that the easiest way to get your children to practise mathematical skills and to develop mathematical understanding is by disguising that practice in a game. Mental arithmetic, logic, probability, properties of shape and space, patterns, networks, systematic working and more can all be taught and reinforced through games. Once a year, Mum would give her students an assignment to design and create their own games. These prototypes would pass through our house for assessment … and that meant being played with.

My father gets bored very easily and uses two main strategies to manage this. Firstly, he creates very structured, optimised routines, so that a dull task happens in the most efficient manner. For example, in about 1983 he wrote a computer programme that, when he types in items needed from the supermarket, will order them according to the layout of the shop. This reduces time spent backtracking and gets the task done in the most time- and energy-efficient manner. Although Dad now lives in a different town, with a different shop, he still uses the programme weekly. And, yes, Tesco does insist on moving everything around every now and then, at which point the programme is rewritten. Secondly, he gamifies life. A favourite obsession of his is to use random generation to 'keep life interesting'. This can be fun: randomly selecting meals for the week or the next CD to play. It can also be frustrating: his wife, my stepmother, was once forced to phone her Uncle Norman because his name came up on the random family phone calls spreadsheet. But it can go too far. My mother was once subjected to an underwhelming week-long holiday in Swepstone in Leicestershire because of random numbers being applied to the index of the *Gazetteer of British Place Names*. In 43 years, neither of them has been back. It's good to find ways for games to become part of your life, but not ways for them to determine the destination of your holidays!

So as a child, board game design and gamification were familiar concepts. When we got bored with the standard versions of games we owned, my sister and I would modify them to mix things up a bit. New character cards and new rules were created for *Guess Who*. *Happy Families* were much happier with great-grandmas, grand-nieces and second cousins twice removed. The code-breaking classic *Mastermind* was more challenging with five or six pegs. Mum says her copy of *The Great Game of Britain* still contains our customised event cards, involving much more outlandish, unusual and (frankly) revolting events than the standard version does.

Our favourite game was **Railway Rivals**. Mum heard of it in an article written in around 1984 by a maths teacher who had used the game to teach his bottom set maths groups.[1] Its designer, David Watts, a maths teacher himself, self-published the game and, in order to get a copy, Mum wrote to him, enclosing a cheque. The game arrived in the post in the cardboard tube in which it still lives all these years later. In the game, players firstly construct their own railway by drawing lines with dry-wipe pens from hexagon to hexagon across a map. In the second half of the game, they run trains on the lines they've created. I recently conducted an extended family audit and discovered that, over five households, we have 32 different *Railway Rivals* maps, including three copies of South Sweden, four copies of London and Western and one prized copy of J. R. R. Tolkien's Middle Earth that none of us knew my sister Jenni owned. Although *Railway Rivals* won the 1984 Spiel des Jahres, a prestigious German award given to the game of the year, it was never mainstream. Even after winning the award, it remains obscure and undiscovered even by the keenest gamers. A far cry from most family games of the time, *Railway Rivals* allowed you to create your own network from scratch, creating a unique board for every game. The flexibility and creativity that *Railway Rivals* allows has hugely influenced my attitude towards board gaming.

My mum also says that she wanted us to learn how to lose. Both my parents would play to win. There may have been handicapping built into the house rules for a few games, but once this had levelled the playing field, it was everyone for themselves. This gave us plenty of chances to fail. I'm sure I didn't always handle losses with grace, but when I won, I knew I had earned it. House rules allowed us to compete as equals. My parents enjoyed playing just as much as we did. Parental enthusiasm rubs off on children and I'm sure I have my parents to thank for sparking my delight in board games.

I was also blessed with a wonderful granny, who lived with us for my entire childhood in a granny flat attached to the house. Every evening my sister and I would each take a turn with Granny. Daily turns lasted around 20 minutes. Sometimes Granny and I would chat, but usually we'd play word games and card games: Beat Your Neighbour, Go Boom, Whist, *Town and Country*, Consequences, Boxes … Granny taught me lots of versions of Patience, to help me entertain myself more effectively. Granny would never have anything planned or something more important to do; she would always just be there ready to do whatever we wanted - for 20 whole minutes. When I'd used up my Granny time and nobody else wanted to play with me, I'd execute full games of *Monopoly* with my cuddly toys - me taking turns for each of them. I'd usually win. My toys were kind to me.

---

1   Unfortunately, I've been unable to track down the source.

As an adult, I've always worked with teenagers in some way or another. In my early twenties, I worked at a summer camp in upstate New York, became a director for a children's theatre company, ran after-school drama groups, spent nine months working as a teen activity coordinator on a cruise ship and eventually became the head of drama in a secondary school. Throughout all these jobs, I modified and designed loads of games to aid my teaching and to keep the teens in my care entertained. I created drama games based on fractions and decimals, scavenger hunts that involved a series of mini logic problems and complex trust games that involved mazes and programming actions.

From 2004 to 2017, alongside my husband, Paul, I was owner and director of Pivotal Education, the UK's largest team of school behaviour specialists. Pivotal Education helps school leaders to define and build positive cultures in their school, improve relationships and embed exceptional behaviour. Pivotal Education has helped thousands of teachers to transform their classrooms and improve outcomes for their learners. My understanding of behaviour and experience of helping teachers to change their own behaviour to impact that of their learners helps me to understand the challenges that parents face in managing behaviour in the home.

In the early days of Pivotal Education, I ran training sessions for primary school teachers in how to teach maths more actively. These sessions would use drama and gamification to challenge them to expand their practice and to take more risks to increase pupils' engagement with the subject. These workshops fired up my mathematical interest, which had been lying dormant since completing my A levels, and I embarked on a second part-time undergraduate degree with the Open University. Six years on, I've nearly completed my BSc in mathematics. I keep getting side-tracked, because the course content provides such great inspiration for board games that I have to go off and make them.

I've been a board-gaming teenager and a board-gaming teacher of teenagers, and now I am a board-gaming parent of one teenage son and another who soon will be. Other people feed their children hearty and varied meals; I feed mine board games. They do get food too (and reasonably healthy stuff), don't worry, but I aim to nourish their souls with games. I realise I'm more than a little obsessed, but games have had such a positive impact on the family that, for me, it is a total no-brainer. Board games are part of our family brand and that's a badge we all wear proudly. I recently overheard my younger son telling my older one that he can only have a new girlfriend on one important condition: she must like playing games. My elder son agreed.

Now I'm putting my understanding of behaviour, my experience with gami-fication, my teaching skills and my game-playing history to use by helping other parents to introduce board games into family life.

WHY BOARD GAMES?

So why board games? There are other ways to engage teenagers in family activities. Other hobbies do exist. You could construct model aircraft, strip and rebuild a car engine, play basketball or do scrapbooking … But board games are different; they are special. Here's why:

- The bar to entry is very low. You don't need special training or certification. Board games don't rely on any special skills or expertise and you don't need to have played a hundred different games to be able to teach someone how to play one. Most games are designed to be picked up, learned and played quite quickly by those who have never touched them before. While you may come across some real board game geeks, you certainly don't have to be one to join in.

- There is a huge amount of variety within board gaming. The types of experience you have while playing games, the differences in mechanics, themes, artwork, characters and components are truly mind-boggling. Games vary in length and complexity. Different games require different skills and knowledge for success. There are games to suit everyone.

- Board games are portable and easy to store. You don't need to take over the loft, as you might with a miniature railway set. You can grab a game from the cupboard and set it up in minutes.

- There is no major long-term commitment. Adults may have grand plans about huge projects to embark on with their children, but even when initially greeted with enthusiasm, the project may easily outlive a teenage attention span (and possibly an adult one too). One rainy day of trying to build a treehouse might be the beginning and end of a gloriously billed parent–child project. Board games have no such issue; each play is a complete experience in itself.

- Board gaming is an indoor pursuit. In the UK it rains. And for months of the year it gets dark early. You may love mountain biking as a family, but it isn't always weather-appropriate. On those long, dark, wet evenings, board games will not let you down.

- Board games will fit into your day. You can select the game according to the number of players you have and the time you want to spend. You can select a game that you can play in half an hour or that takes a full afternoon. Set-up time is minimal. You can grab a game and be up and running quickly.

- Once you own a game, you can play it over and over again: it's an unlimited resource. You aren't restricted to a certain number of plays before the game becomes useless. So if you launch into a game and you're not feeling it, you can pack it away and pick another, with no wastage and no cost.

- Board games increase interaction and boost relationships.[2] When you play games, players focus on one another, but within the safety and structure of the game. To be successful, you learn to communicate effectively so that you can accomplish your objectives.

- Playing games can increase your awareness of others. Players learn to truly listen to obtain information about other players. The timbre, pitch, tone and volume of the voice gives indications of how they are feeling about their moves. A player's body language – like switching the order of the cards in their hand, or becoming unnaturally still, or the direction of their gaze – gives micro-clues to their possible next plays and overall strategy.

- Board gaming is inclusive. Anyone can play. All ages can play together. Many disabilities can also be catered for. Children can compete on a level playing field with their parents. With the right games, strength, age, physical ability and prior knowledge will give you no discernible advantage.

- Playing games improves memory formation[3] and cognitive skills,[4] increases processing speed,[5] develops logic and reasoning skills,[6]

2   Lawrence Robinson, Melinda Smith, Jeanne Segal and Jennifer Shubin, The benefits of play for adults, Help Guide [blog] (November 2018). Available at: https://www.helpguide.org/articles/mental-health/benefits-of-play-for-adults.htm.
3   'Nothing lights up the brain like play. Three-dimensional play fires up the cerebellum, puts a lot of impulses into the frontal lobe – the executive portion – helps contextual memory be developed.' Stuart Brown, 'Stuart Brown: play is more than fun', TED.com [video] (12 March 2018). Available at: https://www.youtube.com/watch?v=HHwXIcHcTHc.
4   Health Fitness Revolution, Top 10 health benefits of board games, Health Fitness Revolution [blog] (15 May 2015). Available at: http://www.healthfitnessrevolution.com/top-10-health-benefits-board-games/.
5   Allyson P. Mackey, Susanna S. Hill, Susan I. Stone and Silvia A. Bunge, Differential effects of reasoning and speed training in children, Developmental Science, 14(3) (2011): 582-590.
6   Jennie Pennant and Liz Woodham, Developing logical thinking: the place of strategy games, NRICH Maths (November 2013). Available at: https://nrich.maths.org/10019.

improves critical thinking,[7] boosts spatial reasoning,[8] improves verbal and communication skills,[9] increases attention and concentration,[10] teaches problem-solving,[11] develops confidence[12] and improves decision-making.

- Playing games teaches competitiveness within a limited domain. The family learns to play to win but they don't *need* to win. Everyone gets used to experiencing defeat; games involve failure on a manageable scale.

- Playing games can increase our consideration of and respect for others. A common parental mantra is, 'You wouldn't like it if your sister did that to you' and with the fast pace of turn-by-turn action in board games, your children can see the implications of this phrase being played out in real-time. 'Treat your brother as you want him to treat you' has a lot more meaning if the tables are going to turn in the next 30 seconds. Through games we learn to consider the impact of our actions on others.

- Board games provide players with challenge. We strive to improve our own performance by experimentation. Mistakes are remembered and learned from. While beginner's luck may occur from time to time, usually players who have had the most experience at playing a game will be the most successful. Players learn that the time taken on refining their strategy and game play will reap benefits in the future.

7 Gwen Dewar, Board games for kids: can they teach critical thinking? *Parenting Science* [blog] (n.d.). Available at: https://www.parentingscience.com/board-games-for-kids.html.
8 Shen-Li Lee, How to help children develop spatial reasoning skills, *Figur8* [blog] (8 February 2017). Available at: https://www.figur8.net/2017/02/08/developing-spatial-reasoning-skills/.
9 John Leana, Sam Illingworth and Paul Wake, Unhappy families: using tabletop games as a technology to understand play in education, *Research in Learning Technology*, 26 (2018). Available at: https://journal.alt.ac.uk/index.php/rlt/article/view/2027.
10 https://www.scholastic.com/parents/kids-activities-and-printables/activities-for-kids/arts-and-craft-ideas/benefits-board-games.html
11 Damian Corless, Teaching life skills using board games? It's child's play ... *Independent.ie* (1 November 2010). Available at: https://www.independent.ie/life/family/learning/teaching-life-skills-using-board-games-its-childs-play--26790410.html.
12 Jean Rhodes, 10 reasons mentors should play cards with their mentees, *The Chronicle of Evidence-Based Mentoring* [blog] (12 April 2015). Available at: https://www.evidencebasedmentoring.org/play-cards/.

■ Playing games has proven health benefits[13] as it induces laughter[14] and reduces stress, which boosts the immune system and lowers blood pressure.[15]

All this potential from a few dusty boxes lurking at the back of a cupboard.

You may come to this book with preconceptions about board gaming. Unless you have played some of the new games that have been published in the last few years, these will likely come from your own experiences of board gaming as a child. But the world of board games is very different now. The rise of crowdfunding has had a huge impact on tabletop games, sparking a surge in innovation and allowing hobby game designers to get their creations out into the world. In the same way that social media has driven a shake-up of traditional journalism, so has crowdfunding forced the big game publishers to get creative. This isn't a renaissance of board gaming; it has *never* been this good.[16] Inventive mechanics, clever interactions, interesting themes and beautiful components will draw you in and get you hungry for more. If you go to a game convention or a specialist game shop, you'll see people from every walk of life. Board gaming is magnetic and indiscriminate in its attraction. It's time to banish your assumptions and get ready for the ride of your life.

WHY NOW?

It seems that everyone is spending more time on their smartphones or other devices and less time communicating face to face. Young people are growing up in increasingly digital environments and some are suffering from reduced social skills, difficulty sleeping and, in some cases, technology addiction. As adults, we too turn to screens for our entertainment and relaxation. There are families all over the country in which people are sharing experiences with their smartphones, rather than with each other. Children are growing up in a world in which this is the new normal. But it seems

13 Alessandro Viggiano, Emanuela Viggiano, Anna Di Costanzo, Andrea Viggiano, Eleonora Andreozzi, Vincenzo Romano, Ines Rianna, et al., Kaledo, a board game for nutrition education of children and adolescents at school: cluster randomized controlled trial of healthy lifestyle promotion, *European Journal of Pediatrics*, 174(2) (2015): 217–228.

14 Lawrence Robinson, Melinda Smith and Jeanne Segal, Laughter is the best medicine, *Help Guide* [blog] (November 2018). Available at: https://www.helpguide.org/articles/mental-health/laughter-is-the-best-medicine.htm.

15 See http://www.healthfitnessrevolution.com/top-10-health-benefits-board-games/.

16 Mason Boycott-Owen, After books and vinyl, board games make a comeback, *The Observer* (13 May 2018). Available at: https://www.theguardian.com/lifeandstyle/2018/may/12/millennials-drive-board-games-revival.

obvious that it shouldn't be normal. How long should we let this go on before we look back, assess the real damage and understand the cost?

It feels like every week a new study emerges warning about the consequences of our children's reliance on smartphones: from social isolation to concentration problems, bullying, bad language and exposure to pornography. Children as young as 12 are eligible for treatment for gaming addiction on the NHS.[17] The World Health Organization has officially classified 'gaming disorder' as a disease,[18] and we have heard that the more time people spend on social media, the lonelier they are likely to become.

Technology is here to stay. We aren't going to reverse back to a 'simpler time' nor would most of us want to. Development will speed up, not slow down. What needs to change is our relationship with technology: our reliance on it and our life outside of it. We need to find ways to manage digital technologies around our relationships, not the other way around. Dr Richard Graham, consultant in digital psychiatry at Nightingale Hospital, runs the UK's first technology addiction service. He says, 'Clearly new technologies are not just blindly positive for all,[19] and critically, knowing when not to use devices may be a cornerstone to digital-wellbeing.'

Today, the majority of parents will have grown up before the internet, the rise of smartphones and the ubiquity of Wi-Fi. When we were growing up, we had to entertain ourselves, make our own fun and experience boredom. But this was a while ago and many of us have forgotten how we used to entertain ourselves, how we discovered information and how we communicated with friends. Today's young adults were born into a time when the internet was mainstream. They've not known a different world. In a very short space of time, all parents will be of the internet generation. Nobody will have even those hazy and rose-tinted memories of life before widespread technology. If we, today's parents, don't make an effort to create rich offline experiences for our families, how will our children be able to do the same for their own children when they are parents? As the bridging generation – who were children pre-internet and parents with-internet – we are in a unique position to challenge and define the new world order. We can't stop the march of technology, but we can establish its place within our families.

17 *The Telegraph*, NHS to treat child gaming addicts as young as 12 isolated from friends (31 July 2018). Available at: https://www.telegraph.co.uk/news/2018/07/31/nhs-treat-child-gaming-addicts-young-12-isolated-friends/.
18 See https://www.who.int/features/qa/gaming-disorder/en/.
19 Richard Graham, A cure for the fear of missing out? *Huff Post* [blog] (22 May 2016). Available at: https://www.huffingtonpost.co.uk/dr-richard-graham/fear-of-missing-out_b_7349230.html.

Fear and panic may help us to educate our children about the perils of the online world, but it won't teach them the joys of the offline one.

As parents, we recognise the problem, but many of us don't know how to shift the balance – so, to start with, it is time to be honest with ourselves about our own relationship with technology. It isn't fair to expect our children to withdraw from screens when we ourselves don't even go to the toilet without our smartphone. There may be a nagging voice in my head that tells me that I shouldn't be on mine, but there is a louder voice that pipes up with all sorts of justifications. If you pine for screen-free time for your family, you should start with yourself. While you read this book and test out the ideas, put yourself through a gentle digital detox. (Have a look at *How to Break Up with Your Phone* by Catherine Price for starters.[20]) Gradually change your relationship with your smartphone so that you are in control of it, rather than the other way around.

You, as a parent, are the best person in the best position to teach your children how to fully live outside their smartphone, tablet or games console. We need to develop our family's offline lives to keep pace with our online ones.

YOU ARE NOT ALONE

Most teenagers develop what their parents would (politely) describe as an over-reliance on their smartphones, creating a refuge into which they can retreat for many hours. Much of the time, they are living within their online worlds. When they are forced out of this world and back into ours, where the structures, hierarchies and rules are different, sparks can fly.

You're not alone; managing children's interaction with their online world is reportedly the biggest issue for modern parents:

Action for Children's latest research has found that nearly a quarter of parents struggle to get their children to "unplug" and take part in activities away from television, smartphone and computer screens. When asked which behaviour they found most difficult to control in their children, more parents said they struggled to limit technology-based activity

---

20 Catherine Price, *How to Break Up with Your Phone: The 30-Day Plan to Take Back Your Life* (London: Trapeze, 2018).

(23 per cent) than get children to eat healthily (19 per cent), go to bed (18 per cent), or do their homework (10 per cent).[21]

The battles that you are having are being played out in households every-where. You may not realise how widespread the issue is because many parents choose not to talk about it. A child's dependency on their smart-phone (or other screens) may be seen as a parenting issue, or even as a parenting failure. Along with the worry about the amount of time spent online goes the guilt that you should be more effective at reducing it. Guilt or embarrassment can prevent parents from openly sharing their concerns with others. So take heart, this is a problem that almost all parents have to deal with. What you may not realise is that you are already *way* ahead of the others in starting to find a long-term solution. By the time you get to the end of this book you will have the understanding and practical strategies you need in order to reconnect with your children through board gaming and begin to balance your family life.

Time passes quickly. It is so important that we try to make the most of the time we have with our children while they are still at home. It is a common family scene to find everyone (including the parents) gazing at their own small screen, but when each person is engaged in their own online world, fewer shared memories are being made in the offline one. If this is true almost every time the family meets, how can you foster a sense of family belonging? Through shared experience we strengthen our relationships and create memories.

Getting caught up in the day-to-day routines and battles stops parents from taking the time to draw the line and make a change. You're not going to do that anymore. There is never a perfect time, but you don't need a perfect time. Follow the strategies in this book and you'll make the change despite the tiredness, the hectic activity and the demands of being a parent.

Most advice about reducing screen time seems to revolve around enforcing restrictions. Keep all smartphones in the kitchen overnight, have prescribed screen-free downtime at least an hour before bed, impose limits on screen time, make sure that there are no phones at the table, etc. Practical advice on what you should do to plug the gaping screen-sized hole left in the fabric of family life is much thinner on the ground. Well, I'll tell you now, restricting screen time won't work. I'll say it again because it's important. Restricting

---

21 *Action for Children*, 'Unplugging' from technology (6 January 2016). Available at: https://www. actionforchildren.org.uk/news-and-blogs/whats-new/2016/january/unplugging-from-technology/.

screen time won't work. In itself, it isn't a solution. The feeling of needing to spend time online, in one's own digital world, is very strong. This feeling, which will drive your children to creatively bypass restrictions or just harangue you until you give up, is so strong that you are fighting a losing battle before you even start. This path will lead you to a world of arguments, suspicion and lies – not the kind of family environment that you yearn to create. Don't get me wrong, restrictions can work, especially when partnered with using screen time as a reward rather than a right,[22] but not in isolation. If you can offer something more important to focus on, then introducing restrictions will be easy. Until that point it will always be hard work. Your job is to work on making your family's *offline* world irresistible. Hook them in using stealth tactics until they are smitten and then watch as the smartphones lie abandoned and unnoticed in another room.

This book will guide you in how to develop a family that plays together. It will open your eyes to the huge impact that play can have on the strength of your family's relationships and the quality of the time you spend together. It won't happen all at once. There'll be times when nothing much seems to be happening. But there will come a day when your kids will come home from school, throw down their bags and beg you to get off your laptop and play a game with them. Patience will pay off. You may need to read this book more than once. Use it as a resource and a guide. When there has been a messy explosion and you are loudly reminded (which you will be) that you are stupid, that this game stuff is stupid and that the whole family is stupid, return to the book. You may find something you missed the first time, something that will be the hook for your child. You'll know it when you find it.

Remember, you're already way ahead of most parents.

Get excited: life is about to change.

---

22 See Noël Janis-Norton, *Calmer Easier Happier Screen Time* (London: Yellow Kite, 2016).

CHAPTER 1

DISRUPT YOUR THINKING

Home truths to get to grips with.

The amount of information and advice that is thrown at us when we become parents is enormous. It can often seem like any decision we make is the wrong one. There is always someone ready to criticise or contradict, usually armed with a barrage of stories to back up their point of view. Doubt and guilt go hand in hand with parenting. As children grow, the challenges change. Dealing with teens and pre-teens can feel like we are navigating our way through a minefield, blind.

But, as a parent, you know your children better than anyone else and you are the person who is the most qualified to bring them up. Gather information, listen to advice, but make your own decisions about what will work with your family in your home. Be confident with your choices, even if those around you are making different ones.

To help you make parenting choices that will enable you to reclaim family time and play more together, here are my home truths. Grasp these and you'll pull your family closer rather than drifting apart as your children mature.

HOME TRUTH 1: THE WAY YOU USED TO PARENT WON'T WORK NOW

Parenting needs to grow as our children do. Children have a way of going through rapid bursts of development, particularly when they hit puberty, and these changes can sneak up on parents and catch us unawares. It is really hard to let go of how we used to parent, especially if we've been successful in the past. Therefore, it is important to be as reflective and self-aware as possible.

When children are young, they rely on us for everything. The parent is their main guide and provider of information about the world and how to operate within it. Younger children tend to believe what their parents say, display less scepticism and are more easily influenced. Most younger children look up to their parents, and adulthood is often revered as a pretty exciting and magical existence.

As children get older, we give them more of an insight into the reality of adult life; we share our weaknesses, fears, worries, responsibilities and concerns. Of course, we must do this to teach them life skills and to help them become rounded, considerate people, but it removes some of the mystery around adulthood and the reverence often diminishes with it. It is hard to retain the control that many parents fight for when you're dealing with young adults who have a wider social network that provides them with external influences on their behaviour and values. This fight between control and independence causes lots of problems in many families.

The desire for independence pushes children away from their parents. Although this is a natural part of growing up, it is often hard for parents to live with. They seem to want to talk, only not to us. As they start to build their own personal lives, they become more secretive and private. Of course, this independence is combined with the fact that they believe they've already learned everything you have to teach them, so they are less open to discussion and advice. Of course, some teenagers are more, well, teenagery than others. Most fluctuate, even in small ways, between wanting to be part of the family and wanting everyone to just leave them alone.

So, as parents of teens or pre-teens, what can we do to make the road a bit smoother and to keep the relationship strong, even in murky hormonal waters? People with adult children often talk about 'coming out the other side'. After the distance and tumult of the teenage years, the bond between parent and child strengthens again. Focusing on the long-term relationship and seeing teenage behaviour for what it really is can be enormously helpful to a harried parent. Deal with the issues with as much detachment as possible and save your emotion for showing your hormonal children love. Look for opportunities to be proud. Look for ways to reinforce how important they are. They might think all sorts of things about you, but never let them think that you don't love them.

HOME TRUTH 2: YOU'LL NEVER GET YOUR CHILDREN TO TELL YOU ABOUT THEIR DAY

Parenting older children is particularly challenging. Communication becomes less open and relationships more strained as they strive for more freedom without yet having any of the tools with which to achieve independence. You keep trying to communicate, but it often feels like you're spiralling further away from each other. You long for the ease with which you communicated when they were younger.

This is how the separation spiral takes hold:

1   The child chooses to spend less time with their parents than they used to, so the parents are not as involved in their day and they don't have as many natural opportunities to chat.

2   The parents become more disconnected with their child's life, but they yearn for more connection and more time to talk. Whenever the parents get the opportunity, they will 'show interest' in their child's life, usually by asking them lots of questions about their day, their friends, their teachers, etc.

3   The child finds this interaction annoying and possibly boring, getting frustrated because their parents ask them the same questions seemingly every time they meet. The child goes quiet and grunts.

4   The adult pads out the silence by talking about their own day, trying to find something to interest their offspring.

5   The child rolls their eyes, while simultaneously checking their smartphone, then makes a hasty exit to avoid having to answer annoying questions and listen to their parents' inane babble about their pitiful lives.

6   Later at dinner, the child launches into a monologue about the intricacies of some video game they are playing, or performs an entire YouTube play-through video word-for-word with a full range of accents and sound effects.

7   The parents roll their eyes and tell the child to stop filling their head with useless information. They then comment on how well they'd be doing at school if only they put the same time and application into their studies as they do into their useless screen-based pastimes.

8   The child looks at the parents incredulously and with a pronounced sneer. They inwardly marvel at their parents' ability to constantly put a

downer on everything. They grumble about how nobody understands them anymore. The child vows to talk less and spend less time with their parents and more time talking to friends who do understand them.

9 Return to Step 1 and continue.

And so the cycle perpetuates and our children spiral ever further away. We ask our children about their lives because we want them to know that we care, but young adults don't always want to say the sorts of things we want to hear. To maintain positive connections with our more stereotypical teenagers, we need to break the vicious cycle.

Rather than trying to get our children to tell us about their day, we need to create more moments in the day when we are doing things together, rather than just talking. When we are doing things, we can talk about the task at hand rather than attempting to find common conversational ground. Many families hold onto the idea of eating together as being the key to maintaining good bonds and open communication. But it is easy to fall into the separation spiral of asking the same questions and giving the same responses. For my family, eating together isn't as important as playing together.

How much time do you spend with your children in an average week? I mean *actually* spend with them. If you are sitting in the same room but absorbed in your own activities, that doesn't count. If you are sitting in the car next to each other, but they have their headphones on and the music turned up loud, that doesn't count (not even if you are talking to them). Watching them doing their swimming practice from the relative comfort of the spectators' balcony doesn't count either. To count as time spent together, you must be choosing to do the same thing, at the same time, in the same space, together. Work it out. Now subtract any time that you spent together on screen-based activities (watching TV or a film, playing video games, etc.) – when your focus was on the screen, not on each other. Now you have your magic number of hours or minutes you've really spent with your children. We're going to work on improving that number.

HOME TRUTH 3: YOU CAN'T CONTROL YOUR CHILD'S SCREEN TIME

The smartphone can be a real bone of contention between parents and children. The energy that goes into angling to get one in the first place, the gradual wearing down of parental resolve with horror stories of stranded phone-less children and bemoaning their status as social pariahs, followed by the all-consuming digital love affair that demands all their attention and time – these slim supercomputers can feel like a grenade launched into the centre of your family. Everyone has an opinion on the use of smartphones, their importance and their place in families and in the universe in general: many people share these opinions freely and sometimes loudly. Criticism and advice flies around whether you've asked for it or not and, as a parent, it is easy to feel that whatever decisions you make will be the wrong ones. There will always be someone with a different opinion to you. Try to work out what you think is best for your family and zone out the haters.

You will never be the only influence on your child's use of technology. They only have to walk down the street, sit on a bus or eat in a restaurant to see a sea of people staring blankly at tiny screens. Unless you home-educate your children, and thoroughly vet their interaction with others, you're not going to be able to construct a childhood free from smartphones. In most families, the adults provide the first model. Adults are just as likely to feel attached to and reliant on their smartphones as young people are, and within a 24-hour period may spend just as much time on them (or more). Beware imposing rules on your children that you have no intention of keeping yourself. Not only will this seem unfair, but it will also undermine the importance of the message. If you want your children to charge their smartphones in the kitchen and not in their bedroom, then you need to do this yourself too. Your reasoning about disturbed sleep and the brain needing to wind down is weakened or totally negated if you seem unconcerned about your own quality of sleep. A rule about no phones at the dinner table should apply to the adults as well. Checking the BBC News website or replying to work emails doesn't make the adult's use of their smartphone more valid. If some-thing is important enough for you to have a rule about it, the rule should apply to everyone.

It is a myth that young people only use their smartphones for social media and mindless gaming. This may certainly be part of their smartphone usage, in some cases a big part, but this is not the beginning and end of the story. Ask your children what they use their smartphones for and you'll start to build up a better picture. For many, listening to music will be the single biggest use. Just as adults may have the radio playing as we are doing other things, our children will be connected to streaming services and broadening their musical appreciation. They may be listening to podcasts or half-watching videos while doing homework, hanging out with friends or tidying their rooms. The smartphone may be present without having their full attention. Our children also use their smartphones to access productivity apps, homework portals, calendars and reminders, photo editors, voice recorders, video cameras, flashlights, alarms and stopwatches, maps, review sites, calculators, cloud storage, pedometers and activity trackers, quizzes, password keepers, e-book readers and so on. Removing the smartphone removes access to more than social media. Smartphones give older children freedom and security.

That said, we all know that social media can be a big problem. This is often the cause of young people feeling that they need to be on their smart-phones at certain times. Some groups of teenagers will communicate more often than others and there isn't much that you can do as a parent to influ-ence the frequency and manner of group communication. You can choose to intervene in your child's online participation within the group, but even if you block certain apps, remove the smartphone at certain times of the day or take a sledgehammer to the thing, the group will continue to communi-cate - without your child. Herein lies a problem. Yes, you could speak to other parents, but you know how hard it is to make a positive change with your own child, so convincing other parents to join you and then expecting them all to be successful is most likely a pipe dream. Save your energy for your own family. So how do you deal with your child's involvement in very busy online networks of friends? That is a hard one and, spoiler alert, I don't have a solution.

Young people often worry about missing out on things, so while the group is talking, they are paying attention and staying involved. Face-to-face con-versations in school are often extended online and vice versa. Some in-joke that has developed one evening may be repeated ad nauseam the following day, making anyone who missed the discussion last night feel a little excluded. To add to the trouble, peak online talk time for teenagers usually seems to be after 9pm. Everyone is back at home after various activities, dinner is over, the world is online. I'm not trying to make a case for unlimited smartphone use, by any means, but it is important that we truly grasp why smartphones are so important to our children. Having this understanding helps us to make decisions about their use within the home, to support our children to make sound choices, to maintain open discussions within the family and to find ways to establish screen-free time. Claiming not to understand the youth of today is not a good starting point. If you really don't understand their motivation, take the time to find out. Ask your own or other people's children and try to see things through their eyes. This will be far better than asking the opinion of other adults.

A 2016 poll revealed that more than 50 per cent of teenagers think they are addicted to their smartphones.[1] The number of parents who felt their children were addicted was only slightly higher. This tells us that many young people have a reasonable awareness of the time they spend online, even if they haven't found ways to reduce it. Social connection and the feeling of belonging to a group, pleasure from receiving 'rewards' in the form of notifications or messages, and validation or recognition from others are heady drugs that fuel this addiction. When the smartphone is the most reliable provider of validation, pleasure, recognition, connection and belonging, it isn't surprising that this most dearly prized possession becomes a crutch to help our children navigate the world.

As they get older, you can't control your child's screen time; they have to learn to control it themselves. Instead of removing this crutch, we need to focus on developing our children's experiences outside of their smartphones, enhancing their social connectivity, validation and sense of belonging in the offline world. Enter the board game.

For the parent trying to encourage their family to play board games, the frustration of repeatedly discovering their children playing games on their smartphone can be monstrous. If they are happy to play games, why is it so difficult to get them to play in real life? Well, playing a game on your smartphone is very easy. Within seconds you have the smartphone out, the game open and you're away. Smartphone games are usually designed to be quick, so the buy-in is minimal. But they are also designed to be addictive, to reward multiple plays and to captivate you with the graphics. They may be easy to start, but they're not so easy to stop.

Games played on smartphones are trend-sensitive. If your son or daughter is seemingly obsessed with a particular game, there is a good chance that all their friends are playing it as well. There'll be competition to get the highest score or to reach the next level before everyone else does. There is a built-in social currency. A board game doesn't have the same sort of pull.

---

1 Kelly Wallace, Half of teens think they're addicted to their smartphones, *CNN* (29 July 2016). Available at: https://edition.cnn.com/2016/05/03/health/teens-cell-phone-addiction-parents/index.html.

It is sometimes hard to stomach that you could have played the whole of *Pandemic Legacy* Seasons 1 and 2 (huge board games that can only be played through once as you destroy and adapt the components while you play) in the 36 hours that they've *wasted* glued to the latest incarnation of *Candy Crush* in the last few weeks. But try not to fixate on this sort of comparison; that way madness lies. If they played less on their smartphone, it doesn't automatically mean that they would magically appear next to you, holding your favourite board game and looking at you with pleading puppy-dog eyes.

As you introduce board games, you're likely to get a bit of kick-back. Older children are often pretty busy – juggling school, homework, clubs, teams and social commitments. You're asking them to give up some of their precious downtime. It may be hard for them to understand the appeal until they experience it themselves. My own children only need to watch someone perform a complex stunt on a YouTube video before claiming that they could do it themselves. The reality is often very different from the perception. Your children might believe that playing board games will be boring, and you might struggle to convince them otherwise until they've actually experienced it. Your children might test your resolve. They may spend quite a lot of time arguing their point, exhaustively. But hold your own.

HOME TRUTH 4: VIDEO GAMES AREN'T AS GOOD AS BOARD GAMES

'I get that you want to spend time with me, but why can't we just play video games together?' Good question, teenaged son. We certainly can spend some time playing video games, but it isn't a patch on playing board games, as you'll soon discover. Don't be swayed. Playing video games together just isn't the same, and here's why:

- **The software may be different, but the hardware is the same.** However stimulating a video game is, all you are doing is pressing the same buttons over and over again … in every game. This is where our unplugged gaming world has a distinct advantage: the hardware changes and our interaction is a physical experience as well as a mental challenge. The advent of virtual reality may totally change the gamer's environment, but the components are virtual, not physical. You can't touch the virtual world (at least not yet).

- **Your focus is different.** When you're playing a video game, everyone's focus is on the screen. But when you play a board game, your focus is on each other. Instead of sitting in a line all facing the same way, you're sitting around a table as a group. Even when sitting next to the person you're playing a video game with, you're not paying attention to them and are unable to pick up on the body language and micro-clues that would indicate their next play.

- **Video games have sound effects and music built in.** This digital sound fills the space and reduces player talk. With board games, you create your own soundtrack of random conversation, laughter, game tactics, diplomatic agreements and blatant bluffing.

- **On the screen you interact with virtual people, not real ones.** Even if you're playing with someone else, you might forget that the person is sitting next to you as you're more concerned with their superpowered digital personification. In the land of board games, you're interacting with real people all the time. Even if players take on the roles of heroes, robots or murderers, they look like themselves and largely behave like themselves. You interact with the people around you, not the game pieces on the board.

- **Most video games don't allow you to pause.** Of course, you can pause the game, but not pause *within* the game. If you break concentration for a second, you may get attacked or miss something vital. Video games are designed to be immersive and to take all of your attention. This total immersion inhibits lateral discussion. You're unlikely to talk about an issue at school or something funny that happened on the bus while present in this all-encompassing virtual world. Most tabletop games enable you to pause at will, weaving your life outside the game into the conversation.

- **Video games are one-dimensional.** Success does not require the use of your voice: you just sit there and wiggle your fingers. To be successful at board games, you need to be able to negotiate effectively, argue your point, win trust, explain strategy, lie convincingly, invent justifications, give cryptic clues and sell your ideas.

- **Video games are location-sensitive.** Board games can be played anywhere and fitted into any bit of time you have. If it is sunny, you can take a game outside. Fancy playing with the neighbours? Just take a game over. On holiday? No problem. No power or internet connection is required.

- **The route ahead has already been designed for you within video games.** Someone has been there before, created this world, allowed you to be in this position and conjured up a solution to enable you to triumph. You can even google your way through the world and find cheats online. In a board game, you are in new territory. Your game may play out totally differently than it has before. You need to use your own powers of problem-solving to deduce the best solution to the problem you're in. Not every circumstance can lead to triumph. Your experience is unique: dependent upon the combination of the people you are with, the game you are playing, your surroundings and the game play.

- **In video games, you have no truly creative powers.** Sure, you can build things that nobody else has built in *Minecraft*, and that can be extremely satisfying, I have to admit. But you can't fundamentally change the building blocks you are given. You can't add new types of materials or interact with them in a way that the game hasn't designed for. Board games are much more basic in their building blocks – usually just made from bits of cardboard and plastic. You can change the rules, add new pieces, create extensions and invent whole new games very easily and with no special skills or technology.

- **Video games create the world for you.** You are experiencing the result of someone else's ideas. Board games allow your imagination to run freer. You expand and create the world in your head and on the table. Much as how reading a book allows you to create an imagined world in your own head in a way that a film never does, so it goes with board games, but even more so. Storytelling and role-playing games in particular allow you to develop full worlds in your head and then interact with real people in that world, exploring together.

So, it is undeniably clear that board games are better than video games! But that doesn't mean that there isn't a place for video games. School is a full-on interactive experience and an onslaught on the senses. Your children may need time to switch off and be on their own. Games played on a smartphone or console are particularly useful to help the brain wind down. Video games help keep children entertained when we are too busy to do so. While we may wish that they'd choose to curl up on the sofa with a copy of *The Hobbit*, or go in the garden and climb trees instead, this idyllic vision of self-occupying children is unrealistic for many families. There is certainly a place for playing video games solo; we just need to make sure it stays in its place.

In fact, you may be able to use video games to help hook your family into board gaming. While you may struggle to get your children to tell you about their day, they are almost certainly quite happy to talk about the video games they are currently playing. They're probably investing time, effort, discussion with friends and a lot of thought into the games they play. Ask them to explain their favourite game, or to show you how it works. Get them to tell you about why they like the game, what events they've enjoyed the most and why they keep playing. Find out whether it is the mechanics, the interactivity, the theme or the characters that give the game its appeal. Learn as much as you can. You can use this information to select board games that offer similar experiences based around themes they enjoy.

HOME TRUTH 5: YOUR DESIRE TO WIN WILL LOSE YOU THE GAME

Board games provide a capsule experience. Each game has rules which must be followed and structures that shape our choices. The boundaries of time and space are clear, and at the end of the game a winner (or winners) will be declared. Each game is a finite experience: from unboxing at the start to re-boxing at the end.

But there is a bigger and much more important game that you need to play: the metagame. The metagame is an infinite game that has few rules, and the rules that do exist are shifting and elusive. The boundaries are not contained, and it is hard to measure your progress. The metagame gives you the reason to play games; it is the motivation and the drive. You play games because you want to spend time with your children. You play games because you want your children to interact and form more meaningful connections with the family. You play games because you want your family's engagement in the offline world to keep pace with their online one. This is the metagame.

Simon Sinek, author and speaker, talks about infinite games and their impact on businesses.[2] His book, *The Infinite Game* - forthcoming at the time of writing - explores his idea that to succeed in business you are playing a game in which the goal, instead of winning, is to keep playing.[3] Getting

2 Simon Sinek, The infinite game [video], *The New York Times Conferences* (31 May 2018). Available at: https://www.youtube.com/watch?v=tye525dkfi8.
3 Simon Sinek, *The Infinite Game: How Great Businesses Achieve Long-Lasting Success* (London: Portfolio Penguin, 2019).

caught up in the small finite games in business – the race to release the next big thing in technology, the desire to win a certain client or complete a huge project – will cause you to make different decisions and distract you from the more important long-term game. The same is true when we play board games with the family. As a parent, if your only focus is on the game on the table, then you lose sight of the reason why you're playing in the first place.

The *need* to win a game will block out all other thoughts. When the desire to win is strong, the decisions you make while playing may be detrimental to the metagame. A parent who is distracted by winning won't notice if the family has stopped enjoying themselves. Memories are long-lasting. If your children don't enjoy the experience, they won't want to play the game again. Some may not want to play *any* game again. You should absolutely play to win, but don't fall into the trap of *needing* to win or you'll lose the much more important metagame.

I encourage you to play the infinite game of strengthening family relation-ships and changing family behaviour. In the process you'll find out about a huge number of finite board games to suit different ages, interests and budgets. But what you'll really be learning is how to play the infinite game – the metagame – how to get the game started and, crucially, how to keep it going.

VICTORY POINTS

- Create opportunities to *show* your teenage children how proud you are and how much you love them.
- Talk to your teenagers about whatever they want to talk about. Feign warm interest in even the most trivial of topics.
- Build more moments into the day in which you are *doing* things with your family, rather than just talking.
- Focus on developing your children's experiences *outside* their smartphones, enhancing their social connectivity, validation and sense of belonging in the offline world.

- Shift from playing video games together, where the focus is on the screen, to playing board games together, where the focus is on each other.

- Put your competitive nature on hold to deliberately and consistently model the behaviours you want to see.

CHAPTER 2

GETTING STARTED

Gently expose your family to the delights of board gaming.

YOUR GAMES COLLECTION

Search your house and gather together all the board games you own. In fact, not just the board games: pick up all the packs of cards, dice, Chess pieces and old Backgammon counters you can find. Go through every room and every cupboard. Check the garage, under the stairs and on top of the wardrobe. Don't forget to check the loft. As you uncover all the games that have been pushed to the back of a dresser or the bottom of a trunk, create a pile of your assorted treasures. You may end up with a few jumbled and incomplete boxes, rather than a huge selection of wonders. That doesn't matter. Whatever you currently have is the start of your collection.

Sort through your miscellany of game bits. Firstly, sift out all the playing cards, dice, counters, sturdy game boards, dominoes and poker chips. These components have multiple uses and will form a key part of your collection. Then look through each board game and check whether it is complete. You'll almost certainly have some games that are missing components or contain items that are in a state of disrepair. Do a good audit of each box and work out what can be saved.

If you have any games that are missing so many pieces that they are really not playable, then you need to perform a 'game strip'. Remove all useful components – for example, counters, resources and tokens. If the board is in good condition, squirrel it away in case you end up with a budding game designer in the house. Sturdy boxes can be used to re-box games that are being held together with ageing sticky tape and string. You could even cut out the artwork from the box and stick it onto another to prolong the game's life. Completely broken pieces and accumulated rubbish can be thrown out, but any game pieces that are intact should be kept in a box somewhere … at least until you've finished reading this book.

Now you need to undertake some repairs and general maintenance. If you're missing cards from a pack, recommission a joker or two. Just grab a permanent marker and write the missing value over the top of the joker (just avoid the few games that involve the actual jokers in the pack). Use your trusty pen to refresh any faded numbers on dice. Patch up the boxes, use counters to replace broken components, wipe down any whiteboards or laminated scorecards, and sharpen or replace pencils. If you have any games that contain bespoke score sheets or game pads, check that you still have a good supply. If you only have a few – or none – left, create your own or download some from the internet. Just google 'printable *Cluedo* sheets', for example, and you'll instantly get a range to choose from. If you have a few originals left, laminate them if you can and get some dry-wipe pens.

When the games are checked, dusted and mended, you'll need to find a new home for your collection. These bits are no longer going to be stored in 15 different places, out of sight and out of mind. Your games are going to become an important element of family life, so they need to be given their own space. Sort out a good size cupboard or set of shelves, ideally somewhere that is accessible for the whole family. Avoid using a space that you can only just squeeze everything into. One way or another, your collection is going to grow. Make a 'Games Cupboard' sign if you want to. You could create one from the broken boxes you're throwing away.

As you're putting the games away in their new home, choose your favourite and keep it out. Put it on the table. Get the board and a few components out if you wish. If you have time, set up the game and play it by yourself. Be all the different players. Play for ten minutes or an hour if you wish; your aim is to get reacquainted with it. Leave it on the table until the family come home. You need not mention the game, but its presence on the table may elicit a few questions or some interest. Show your family the new games cupboard, but don't demand that they play with you. The plan is to tempt them into coming to you, and wanting to play, rather than forcing games upon them. This may take some time, but it will be worth it.

Remember, your objective is to gently increase your family's exposure to board and card games. By sorting out what you already own and giving them their own space, you've already successfully boosted the presence of games in the family and optimised the environment for board gaming.

PLAYING SOLO

Try playing the solo card game Spaces. You can find the rules on *The Dark Imp* blog.[1] At first play, it may seem as if this is a game of pure luck, but there are multiple choices to make about which cards to move first. The order of the moves you make and your decisions about which suit to place on each line have an impact on the outcome of the game. You're likely to start to plan ahead and analyse solutions before you make a move. Play it several times until you're confident with the rules. When you get to the end of round three, make a note of your end position. Each time you play, see if you can improve on your score.

This is a one-player card game. As this is a book about playing as a family, you may be wondering why we are starting here. Well, firstly, playing games needs to become a normalised family activity. For it to be normal for the family, it needs to be normal for you. Playing solo builds up your familiarity with game playing and gives you a base to build on. Secondly, you may *need* to start small. Some parents may be able to skip into the kitchen and merrily call out to the children of the family to put down their smartphones and come and play a game, but for most of us, until game playing is part of normal family life, this approach is unlikely to elicit the response we want. The goal is to make offline time irresistible: something everyone looks forward to, wants, needs and remembers. To get to this point, we have to play the longer game. The first step is raising awareness of traditional games and normalising their presence in the house.

The game Spaces requires a lot of space: a big table or the floor. If you get giant playing cards (readily and cheaply available online) you'll need even more space. Someone walking into the room when this game is being played is going to notice it. I defy anyone, even the snarkiest teenager, not to ask what you're doing and watch for a few moments. Keep playing. Explain what you're doing *if* you're asked. Let them have a go for a bit *if* they want to; stand aside so they can take over; watch and explain what they need to know as they progress. Don't worry if you get less than two minutes of their time or interest. We are just sowing the seeds and some may fall on stony ground. You have to be seen to be enjoying yourself or nobody else will buy in.

When someone is playing with a pack of cards, an observer may be driven to touch and play with the cards too. You're going to use this to your

---

1 Ellie Dix, How to play Spaces patience, *The Dark Imp* [blog] (27 February 2019). Available at: http://www.thedarkimp.com/games-puzzles/spaces-patience/.

advantage. Set yourself up to be discovered. Make sure you seem uncon-cerned about whether your family join you or not. Enjoy playing. Focus on the game, not the child. If a member of your family joins you and takes over your game, you can start up a new game next to them. Have a couple of extra packs of cards ready for this eventuality. You are playing alongside each other, even if you are not yet playing together.

When you think back to your early experiences of board games, what mem-ories come to mind? Endless hours of *Monopoly* on rainy days? Playing *Mouse Trap* at your friend's house? Granny's old *Scrabble* set with the tea-stained board? Do you look back on these memories with fond wistfulness or do you shudder? You only have to mention *Monopoly* in adult company to see a huge range of surprisingly strong reactions. *Mouse Trap* was delightful but also painfully tedious. Granny may have been your escape and refuge, with all the time in the world to offer you, or you might have been forced to visit her and play *Scrabble*.

Your memories and experiences will colour the way you now feel about board games. Try to put these feelings in a box and shelve them for a while. Rose-tinted glasses can be just as damaging as being haunted by ghosts of the past. Fortunately, there are so many brilliant games out there you never have to play *Monopoly* again (unless you want to). You're going to focus on creating new experiences, rather than dwelling on your preconceptions.

Adding to your repertoire of one-player games and playing them in family areas is a useful tactic for hooking the family in, but it does more than that. It hooks you in too. To set up family game nights and make tabletop gaming a normal part of family life, you have to be engaged in it yourself. When you're hooked, your enthusiasm will be infectious.

You should arm yourself with the following basic kit: two packs of cards, six dice and a set of dominoes. Set yourself a challenge to learn ten new one-player card, dice or domino games in the next two weeks. There are some great books available that are packed with options.[2] Browse the different types of games or dive in at random.

Note down the games as you play them and give each a rating. As your range increases, you'll start to identify game mechanics that appeal to you and those which you don't like. Some games are completely luck-based, others allow more decision-making. Some games require memory, others

---

2   I'd recommend David Parlett's *The Penguin Book of Card Games* (London: Penguin, 2008), Reiner Knizia's *Dice Games Properly Explained* (Blue Terrier Press, 2010) or Sid Sackson's *A Gamut of Games* (New York: Dover Press, 2011).

dexterity. If you strongly like or dislike a game, try to work out why. It will help you to select games in the future. Some people also like to keep track of their scores, competing with themselves in subsequent plays.

If you'd like to take solo gaming a bit further, get your hands on a copy of a modern classic, **Pandemic**. **Pandemic** is a multiplayer co-operative game (in co-ops all players work together to beat the game – more about these later). In **Pandemic**, players form a team of specialists fighting the international spread of a deadly infection. If you contain the infection, you win. If the infection becomes uncontrollable, you lose. You can easily play **Pandemic** on your own by controlling all the experts. It is a simple but truly captivating game and the theme and components may attract the family – the infection cubes are particularly pleasing. If you're playing solo **Pandemic**, it is easy for others to jump in and take control of some of the experts. If they want to jump out again, no problem. Make sure that you take the time to learn the rules yourself before you include others. Hide yourself away until you know what you're doing or play when everyone else is out of the house. YouTube is your friend. Search for 'how to play' or 'get started' and the name of the game: there are lots of videos online. Look for videos that are 5–15 minutes long. These will give you the basics in a succinct way, meaning you know enough to get started.

Some games are designed as one-player puzzles. **Rush Hour** requires you to release a little red car from a traffic jam on a 6x6 board. The brightly coloured and very tactile cars must be moved in a certain sequence to free the red car. Similarly **Tip Over** requires crates of different sizes to be tipped over in the right order to allow the red Tipper Man to reach his home crate, and in **Gravity Maze** the player works out where and how to place components so that a silver ball travels from start to finish without dropping out of the maze. With all three of these logic games, the first puzzles are easy, then they get more challenging. Other puzzles, such as **Arokah**, require you to put pieces together in a certain way to construct different shapes. While all these are designed to be played solo, it is easy to work in pairs to solve challenges if any of the family wish to join you. Starting with one-player games and puzzles is a low-risk way of hooking your family in. They can dabble a bit, help with a challenge and then move on. There is no competition, just co-operation.

GAMES ON SHOW

Your games don't all need to be hidden away in a cupboard. Out of sight really can be out of mind. You may not want the bulk out on display, but having a few games and puzzles easily accessible and in full view has a number of advantages:

- **To snatch some extra time with your family.** Leaving *Zombie Dice* on the kitchen work surface might trigger a quick ten-minute battle. If you have a pack of cards on the coffee table, you can deal everyone into a round of Knockout Whist before they've worked out what is happening. We can't always fit in time for full-on game nights. Even in our household, where everyone wants to find time to do this, the rest of life – rugby, swimming, homework, drama – gets in the way. But we can always carve out 15 minutes, particularly if the game is right there in front of us.

- **To normalise game playing.** The visible presence of games helps to make playing games and doing puzzles a routine activity, like eating or getting dressed in the morning. If you have one book of poetry in your house – covered in dust and hidden on a shelf – it would be an abnormal, perhaps even strange, event for someone to pull out the book and start performing poetry in the living room. If there are poetry books all over your house and poems displayed on the wall, this activity would be more normal, expected even. So it goes with games. Leave *Takenoko* on the table and nobody will think it odd when you shove a hungry panda and an exasperated gardener at a child and ask them to grow some bamboo.

- **To increase opportunities for collaboration.** Puzzles like *Rush Hour* and *Arokah* feature lots of different stages to work through. One person can sit and do these puzzles while others wander in and out, help a bit, give some advice and maybe join in for five minutes. Understanding how to work with others is built up over many small experiences. Puzzles enable teamwork in small, low-risk bursts. Yes, arguments might ensue, but they also might not. Arguments are certainly much less likely if the family is used to helping each other with puzzles.

- **To promote interesting discussion.** Games and puzzles are the cognitive equivalent of ear worms (those songs that just get in your head and that you can't stop humming). The concentration, logical investigation and decision-making required for solving puzzles and developing game tactics get in your head. You go over game play, find yourself daydreaming about alternative strategies and, crucially, you make this a topic of conversation in and outside the family. I've been receiving a monthly murder mystery puzzle box from the US – some clues are in the box, others can be found online. The various clues, periodically flung across the dining table, have been picked up and studied by family and friends, leading to discussion, collaboration and, eventually, successful deductions.

To provide an alternative to digital entertainment. To compete with the utter convenience and speed of picking up your smartphone and playing a game on an app, we must make games and puzzles as easily accessible. The most valuable commodity is our attention. Companies spend millions on marketing to get a few moments of our attention – they are brilliant at it. It is easy to get distracted online; time just disappears as we inadvertently follow another advert in disguise. Give your attention something to really focus on, without being distracted by push notifications or diverted by in-app adverts.

To get the brain working. The presence of games and puzzles on display increases the chances that you will pick them up and play with them. In turn, this reduces the amount of time you spend being passive. It is amazing how much of daily life we can sail through without even thinking. Most drivers are used to the experience of arriving at a destination and realising that they can't really remember the journey. We cook, clean, walk dogs and sometimes even do our jobs on autopilot. Good games and puzzles require active attention and lateral thinking.

To develop strategies for trickier games. Some games are quick to teach but take a lifetime to master. Chess is one such example. Tactics are developed over time and through many, many plays. You could designate a small coffee table as the Chess table. Its presence encourages regular play, which helps players to form strategies and understand game play.

And last, but certainly not least:

To reinforce your 'brand' as a game-playing family. Not every family plays board games. Not every family knows how to entertain themselves without screens. Games on display strengthens the message to members of the household that this family is different. This family values time together playing games. There is no better way to broadcast your priorities to visitors and to the wider family than to give games and puzzles prominence around the house. The subliminal messaging is powerful.

DELIBERATE STEALTH

By playing solo puzzles and games in prominent positions around the house, you've begun to use deliberate stealth tactics to influence the behaviour of your family. You're now going to turn this up a notch.

The natural next step is to tackle a two-player game. Select the person in the household who you think is most likely to be receptive. This may be your partner or one of the children. If nobody fits the bill, rope in a friend, a neighbour, or a member of your extended family. Your aim is twofold: firstly, you need to convey the message that games are appealing and really fun, and secondly, you need to normalise the activity within the home. Many games have two-player variants, but some have been specifically designed for two. If you like trick-taking card games, for example, have a look at **Claim** *or* **The Fox in the Forest** for intriguing new twists on the mechanism and beautiful artwork to go along with it. In **Claim**, the suits are factions of goblins, dwarves, knights, doppelgängers and the undead, all with differing abilities that affect whoever wins the trick. The cards you win in the first round become your hand for the second. In **The Fox in the Forest**, odd cards trigger special actions and you're trying to take the most tricks, but if you take too many you end up scoring nothing. The advantage of having some good two-player games in the house is pretty obvious: you only need one other person to play with. In busy households, shared moments between two family members can be rare. Playing a two-player game can enable you to have short bursts of time with individuals, in which your focus is solely on them.

Try **Hive** for an easy to learn but satisfyingly thought-provoking game for two. The chunky tiles, which represent different insects, look good on the table and feel good in your hand. Your aim is to protect your own queen bee while attempting to capture your opponent's by surrounding it on all sides to prevent escape. With all the options on the table and nothing hidden from view, the rest of the family can watch, advise and learn how to play, asking questions openly and taking part in tactical discussion. **Hive** is small enough to sit among the plates and bowls on your kitchen table and robust enough to be played while you eat. Unlike games containing cardboard components, you can't do any damage to the **Hive** tiles. If they get coated in bolognese sauce, just rinse them. You could play one side of the table versus the other; each team making joint decisions about how to move. It doesn't matter if you have uneven teams. During dinner you have a captive audience, so stealthily hook them in while they eat. You could run an experiment. Time how long everyone stays at the table for dinner on a normal day, then time how long they stay when they are playing a game over dinner.

Card games also work really well at the dinner table. You can easily place your hand face down next to your food when you're eating and pick them up again when it's your turn. For many games you don't need much central space, just enough to play tricks or pick up and discard cards. It is also easy to find cheap plastic cards which won't be damaged by sticky fingers. Also try games that 'grow' as you play them. Get hold of a double-twelve set of dominoes to play **Mexican Train**. This game grows from a central node and ends up sprawling all over the table. If you start playing towards the end of dinner, you'll fit it around your plates to start with and then clear them away as you finish eating and the game takes over. While it might be easier to wait until everyone has finished, you'll lose some members of the family as soon as the dinner is cleared away. By overlapping dinner and game time, you're employing deliberate stealth tactics to get maximum participation.

Avoid forcing people to join in. You are the best judge of the tactics to employ with your own children. You may be tempted to put pressure on them to participate because you think they'll love it when they get going, but be careful: this is a dangerous strategy. It is really important to avoid negative game-playing experiences as much as possible. If a member of your family feels strong-armed into joining in and then sits there bitterly plotting their revenge and pointedly snarling at the game play, you'll find it even harder to get them to play next time and everyone else's game will be negatively affected. So don't worry if they choose not to participate. If they watch even a bit of the game during dinner, that is fine. Slowly they may begin to stay for longer and watch a bit more. One day they might offer the odd bit of advice to a neighbouring player and, at some point, they might join in.

Use your two-player games to set up an ongoing competition or tournament for the highest score. Stick a large piece of paper to the wall or balance a corkboard in the corner of the kitchen to display the ongoing scores. The competition board acts as a reminder and encourages participation over a period of time. Players can participate when they wish.

Selecting the right game at the right moment is important. Make sure you have enough time and energy to play the game, because it is really frustrating if you have to pack up when things are getting interesting. The game length on the box may be deceiving, so do a quick search online to see what others say about the time needed. If it is your first shot at a game, allow some extra time as you'll be teaching as you play.

If you're looking to purchase some new games for the family, start with ones that are light but not too light. These 'gateway games' are quick to teach and straightforward to understand, but challenging enough to keep everyone pondering tactics and developing new strategies. Gateway games have good replayability. Nobody wants to waste money on games that aren't going to be played much. Games that scale up well – allowing you to play with different group sizes – will get the most plays. There are so many gateway games to choose from, and picking just a few is difficult, but here are a few that I think are perennial hits:

- *Ticket to Ride.* Race others to construct train lines on a map to complete secret objectives. Each turn you choose to either take cards or play cards to claim a route. Players must decide which routes to prioritise in order to construct their network and connect key cities. There are lots of different versions so make sure you check the player count before buying the game. The Europe and North America maps allow for 2-5 players.

- *King of Tokyo.* Throw dice to battle others, win abilities and become the most powerful monster. This is a fast-paced, dice-rolling, push-your-luck game that rewards players when they enter and stay inside Tokyo. But the risks of attack from other monsters are much greater inside the city. Get out with a healthy number of victory points before you die from the damage you've been dealt. For 2-6 players.

- *Takenoko.* Grow different-coloured bamboo, herd a giant panda and direct an exasperated gardener to complete your own objectives while aiming to prevent others from completing theirs. This is a game that grows as you lay different coloured tiles around a central pond to create a zen garden. Players have individual secret objectives relating to the placement of the tiles, the height of the bamboo and the different colours of bamboo the panda has eaten. For 2-4 players.

- *For Sale.* This superlight game can be explained in three minutes and plays over two quick stages. In stage 1, players bid for houses of varying quality while managing their limited and dwindling supply of cash. In stage 2, players resell their property and try to turn the largest profit. Light strategy mixed with a dollop of luck, this works well for young children and adults. For 2-8 players.

- *Carcassonne.* Lay tiles to create a land of fields, roads, cities and monasteries. Place your meeples (miniature people) in different ways to claim elements and score points. The game starts with just one tile and the land grows as new tiles are added in each turn. It is tempting to grow a sprawling, high-value city but devastating when an opponent performs a hostile takeover. Balance your choices to complete constructions and keep your meeples free for new projects. There are also lots of expansions to extend game play. For 2-5 players.

THE APPEAL OF BOARD GAME COMPONENTS

It is normal to want to touch things. We walk through shops touching things even though we know how they are going to feel. This roots us in a place, even if just for a moment and connects us to the physical world around us. If you see someone else feeling the fabric of a shirt on a rack or taking a mug off a shelf and holding it, you may find yourself following their behaviour. In your home, it is entirely possible that a fly swatter has been sitting untouched on the bookcase for the last two months. If one child picks it up and starts using it, you can bet another will be absolutely compelled to use it immediately too. Arguments might ensue.

Game components are a big hook that can be used to draw young people out of their virtual gaming environment and into the realm of the tabletop world. Think back to the board games you enjoyed when you were a child. I guarantee that some of these stand out in your mind due to the components they came with. When I was a child, we had a game called *Gambler* – my personal favourite by a country mile. I liked the vivid artwork on the game board and the four different stacks of brightly coloured cards. I liked the variety of tasks you could engage in as you moved around the track. I liked the big dollar-sign game pieces and the smaller pawns used for betting. But the jewel in the crown? The dice shaker. Six dice completely encased in a translucent orange plastic shaker. The shaker has a flattish cylinder at one end, in which the dice are shaken, and a long cuboid attached to it, which the dice fall into when upended – displaying them in a certain order. It was a source of pleasure and delight. In fact, it still is.

You don't have to have *Gambler* to experience the delight of great components. The dice popper in *Frustration* turned this annoying and really quite awful game into something to look forward to playing. The intricate plastic bones and pleasing tweezers of *Operation*, the cars in the *Game of Life*, the secretive game boards of *Battleships*, the giant spinner in *Twister* and, of course, the components of *Mouse Trap* all have their rightful place in childhood memories. But now there is a seemingly infinite range of games with intriguing and irresistible components – from the very pleasing gems of the fast trick-taking game **Diamonds**, to the stacking camels of the quirky racing and betting game **Camel Up**, to the laser-shooting pieces of the abstract and strategic **Khet**, to the foam guns of the gangster-inspired, loot-grabbing **Cash 'n Guns**, to the bright yellow airship in **Solenia**, the resource-gathering game of floating cities, to the countless games that involve intricate miniatures – the opportunities to draw the family in with exciting hardware are endless. But the best news of all is that these games are brilliant: they are more than the sum of their fabulous components.

In **Fireball Island: The Curse of Vul-Kar**, players aim to gather treasure as they explore a huge three-dimensional island that rises to a peak where the enormous head of Vul-Kar may be spun to spew lava (marbles) in different directions to send players barrelling down the mountain. Some games use components to develop the landscape as you play. In **Santorini**, players use their god-like powers to create a network of white buildings, reminiscent of the Greek island cliffside town, while **Photosynthesis** allows you to create a woodland of beautiful trees (before you chop them down) to gain points.

You can also add elements to make more traditional or less component-heavy games more tactile. A dice tower is a structure containing hidden platforms into which dice are dropped before they bounce off multiple internal surfaces and roll out at the bottom. Buy or make your own dice tower to add some excitement to simple dice throwing, or invest in personal dice trays so players can throw their dice away from the main board. Put your cards in card sleeves to improve the durability and feel. Design and make your own special game mats using calico or felt. Draw on them with marker pens to make areas for cards, dice and counters. Just because you are 'only' playing Rummy doesn't mean you can't play on the most beautiful game mat.

THE IMPORTANCE OF FAMILY RITUALS

When you think back to the traditions of your childhood, the customs that were repeated time and time again probably stand out in your memory. Big festivals and celebrations usually come with family rituals. When I was a child, bulging pillowcases were laid at the end of our beds on Christmas Eve. These were opened in our parents' room, everyone piled onto the bed, paper everywhere. Then cups of tea, breakfast and more presents by the tree. Grandma would turn up mid-morning, by which time the sherry would be out, and a traditional roast would follow. Christmas afternoon was about wine for the grown-ups and board games for everyone. The rituals I have with my own family are very similar. Your Christmas might look different. You might have a naughty elf-on-a-shelf, special Christmas pyjamas, a brisk after-dinner walk, tipsy charades, *Home Alone* (1, 2 or 3) or A Festival of Nine Lessons and Carols from King's College, Cambridge, as part of your tradition. Your family may not celebrate Christmas, but you will almost certainly have some annual rituals surrounding important days.

But it is not just the big occasions that follow well-formed patterns. There are rituals around many aspects of our lives. To be clear, I'm not just talking about habits. Habits are things we do without thinking, daily occurrences that happen without us noticing. A ritual is a pattern of behaviour or sequence of events that is important to you; something you look forward to and think back on. If you support a sports team, you may well have a ritual around going to watch matches: the clothes you wear, the way you travel, the items you bring with you, the songs you sing, the people you meet up with and the food you eat all play their part. What happens when it snows? Do you make a snowman, go sledging or make snow angels? Maybe you sit in the window with a hot chocolate and marshmallows. Do you have family film nights? Who sits where? Do you have popcorn and blankets? On holiday my husband and children always watch as many *Top Gear* specials as they can fit into the schedule. It is part of our holiday tradition.

Rituals help to build the expectation and anticipation around an event. The reason you look forward to certain occasions is because you have experienced the things that made it special before. You look forward to going to the cinema, not just because you're excited about the film, but because you love the experience of sitting in the comfy seats with a tub of popcorn – even the trailers have their allure. Your family rituals may be completely unique, but even if they are common to many families, they are no less treasured. Visitors to the family are initiated into the rituals and, under your roof, must do it your way. Rituals make common experiences special. Rituals signify importance and create a sense of belonging.

Many of our family rituals revolve around board gaming. Several times a week, the table is cleared and the games mat is brought out. The mat is just a plain black cloth, but vastly improves the game-playing experience in the eyes of the children. The mat is brushed clear of crumbs and fluff and perfectly lined up on the table. Someone organises drinks. Someone else suggests how we are going to select the game. During the game, phones go unanswered; nobody is multitasking. Packing up is communal and often lengthy as post-game analysis begins.

Nikki Bush, a parenting expert from South Africa, talks about the importance of creating a unique family brand. Your 'brand' is the essence of what makes your family special. Bush says that your family brand has three pillars: values, structure and togetherness. She says, 'Rituals are concrete experiences which give them much more power than a lecture from parents about the family values. Children learn best through real experiences that get them personally involved.'[3]

Regular board gaming as a family strengthens each of Bush's three pillars: values, structure and togetherness. Moreover, it is easy to create rituals around playing board games. Each game can be thought of as a structured capsule experience, which can be modified and embellished to create something unique. Even if it's not cool to show it, it is hard for anyone to resist a family ritual, so developing ways to give your game play a special edge will help to draw the family in. Repeated, normalised activities form strong shared family memories.

BOARD GAME RITUALS

To elevate board gaming to a fundamental part of the family identity, introduce some rituals. These rituals can be low-key and designed to make everyone happy and comfortable, or they could be quite elaborate and designed to increase delight, excitement and anticipation around playing the game. If you're struggling to engage your children in board games, you might like to experiment with more unusual rituals that add an element of mystery to the activity, deliberately elevating the status of board gaming within the family.

Here are some rituals you could try:

- **Always sit in the same places round the table.** Perhaps create name cards to go in each place. You could even make these out of spare playing cards. Make place cards for frequent visitors too: grandparents, friends and neighbours.

- **Choose a game-night theme tune.** Play this tune when you are setting up and clearing away. 'Games People Play' by Joe South or 'Play the Game' by Queen, perhaps.

- **Choose a special game-night food, drink or snack combo.** Make this a special treat that you only have on game night. Virgin piña coladas and cheesy goldfish, anyone?

- **Allocate special game-night roles** – for example, bar person, official photographer, reporter, score person, banker … The roles can be

3   Nikki Bush, Parenting tips: why rituals are important in family life, *Nikki Bush* [blog] (19 September 2017). Available at: https://nikkibush.com/rituals-are-important-in-family-life/.

written on counters and placed in a drawstring bag to add an element of randomness to the pre-gaming ritual.

- **Develop some game-night catchphrases.** Make up your own rather than stealing them from gameshows. You could keep a logbook with a tally chart to keep track of who manages to say the catchphrases at appropriate times in conversation each week.

- **Choose a special item of clothing** or an accessory that must be worn during game night. This could be an armband, a hat or possibly special medals.

- **Find a mascot.** The mascot should have a place at the table or on the table. The mascot could have its own pack of cards or set of dice and must, of course, wear appropriate game-night clothing.

Think about it this way: if you were going to set up a sports team, what sorts of things would you do to make the players feel like they belong? Now, I'm not suggesting that you have to create a full kit (and away strip) for game nights, but we can learn from the huddle, the ritual handshakes, the mottos and the songs. These make players feel part of something special, something that matters. These shared experiences create shared memories, continuing to have an impact for many years.

THE GAME CHEST

Part of the importance of rituals is that they *only* happen in a certain situation: the restaurant you only go to on your birthday, the songs you only listen to when you're running or the lucky socks you only wear when you have a big day at work. To create an instant ritual hit at game night, introduce the Game Chest. The Game Chest only comes out on game nights. The rest of the time, it stays visible on a shelf, as a reminder of the wonders of board gaming.

In an ideal world the Game Chest will be kept locked, except when board gaming. So you'll need a lockable chest or box that is eye-catching and intriguing. You might find a pirate-style treasure chest at a car boot sale, or maybe an army-style lock box on eBay. You may even have something old and unusual hidden away in your loft. The Game Chest is the keeper of board-gaming delights and the centre of game-night rituals. If you are feeling creative, you could even start your game night with a hunt for the key. Give the family some clues about where it might be hiding: a riddle, a map of the house with an X marking the spot or a list of directions or instructions.

For a really quick set-up, put the key in the place of a common household item – the toothpaste, for example. Pick up the toothpaste and put that in place of something else, maybe a wooden spoon. Place the wooden spoon where you would normally find the toilet roll. Repeat as desired with other items. Then give the final item to the family for them to work backwards to find the key. Once the key has been discovered, the chest can be opened.

The items that live in the Game Chest are intended to make your game night special. You may have some individual game pawns that belong to each member of the family. These are the pieces that represent the player on the board in a game. My mum gets very upset if anyone else wants to be the iron in *Monopoly* – that is *her* game pawn. Game pawns don't have to be restricted to use in one game only. Forget what is in the box; you can use your own personal game pawn in whatever game you want. Purchase some miniature figures, comb Etsy for custom meeples, go hunting in junk shops for small trinkets or charms, or you could even make your own designs and send them to a custom 3D-printer. If this sounds like too much trouble, raid the *Monopoly* box and choose your favourite classic player piece. Put them in a little bag and store them in the Game Chest.

Here are some other things that could live in your Game Chest:

- Your game-night mascot (to sit on the table and watch the game).
- A gamemaster's hat (as a signifier of this important role).
- An official scorebook (for keeping track of your plays).
- A game journal (for documenting the metagame).
- A visitor book (to collect comments and signatures from non-regulars).
- A selection of game pawns for visitors (so they feel included).
- Dice, playing cards, poker chips and dominoes (all your classic gaming staples).
- Dice shakers, dice trays or a dice tower (to improve the dice-rolling experience).
- Dry-wipe pens (to write on laminated score sheets).
- A calculator (for tricky maths).
- Spare timers (in case you want to impose a turn-taking time limit).
- A game mat (if you favour a smooth, slightly spongy gaming surface).
- A surprise (something unexpected – we have a tin of sardines in ours, although I've no idea why).

Put the key items for your own game-night rituals in the chest. The chest is a focal point that builds excitement and anticipation. Even when it is not in use, make sure it lives in a special place in full view. It is worth putting some time and effort into it, as the Game Chest will most probably go down in family legend. Your children might replicate this with their own children – either creating their own chests or fighting over who the original should be handed down to. You will not just be creating a tradition for your children, but possibly for many generations to come.

VICTORY POINTS

- Immerse yourself in one-player games before drawing the family in.
- Employ stealth tactics to hook the family in without demanding their attention and participation.
- Develop rituals to make game nights your own to increase the sense of family belonging and build the anticipation of playing.
- Define your identity and shape your family brand through the prominence of board games around the house and throughout family life.
- Run interference with screens by making a variety of interesting games and puzzles very easily accessible.

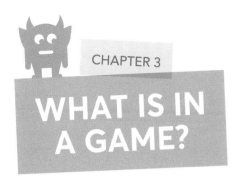

CHAPTER 3

WHAT IS IN A GAME?

Understand the breadth and variety of the hobby.

Throughout this book I mention all sorts of different games. Even though more than a hundred games are mentioned, this is but a tiny scratch of the surface of the huge volume available. As you get drawn into the world of board gaming, you'll discover what sorts of games suit you and your family.

While most of the games mentioned include some element of chance to force players to react to changing circumstances, you'll find few, if any, games of pure luck here. Games of pure luck remove the players' ability to make decisions that will affect the outcome of the game. This lack of influence significantly reduces their interest in the game and their desire to replay it. While younger children may be kept entertained by pure chance, most older children and adults quickly become bored. So almost all of my recommended games involve some level of decision-making and tactics.

Many games revolve around a *theme*. Themes used in board games are incredibly diverse, although some are more common than others. Space exploration, medieval agriculture, zombie apocalypses and civilisation building are prevalent board-gaming topics, for instance. Games without a theme are referred to as 'abstract'. Well-known abstract games include Chess, Backgammon, Draughts and Go. Many traditional games from around the world – such as Mancala and Pachisi – would also come under the category of abstract strategy games.

While it is sometimes useful to categorise games in terms of theme, particularly if you have a special interest in a certain topic, it is generally more helpful to group together games with others that work in the same kind of way. The online encyclopaedia *Board Game Geek* lists 51 different game *mechanics* – which simply means the basic way in which the game works – and offers a concise explanation of each of these.[1] Card games like Whist and Bridge are 'trick-taking' games: each player is aiming to win the trick.

---

1. See https://boardgamegeek.com/browse/boardgamemechanic.

Snakes and Ladders and *Ludo* are 'roll and move' games; you roll the dice, then you move. Trick-taking and roll and move are examples of board game mechanics.

In this chapter, I'll run through some of the main categories, so that you can develop a picture of the range of games available. Please note, this is a whistle-stop tour and in no way designed to be an exhaustive list of game mechanics.

GAMES WITH A STRONG NARRATIVE ELEMENT

Deduction and bluffing games

Deduction games usually rely on players having hidden information, which they use to deceive others. Games of this type often revolve around all players racing to discover the same information. In **Cryptid**, for example, players are cryptozoologists who are all trying to discover the location of the infamous Cryptid. Each player holds one piece of information, which they aim to keep hidden. Only when all the information is pieced together is it possible to work out the location of the beast. Other deduction games work on players discovering different information about their opponents' objectives. **Dead of Winter**, for example, is a post-apocalyptic zombie-themed game in which players work together to achieve a common aim but, in addition, must meet their secret personal winning conditions. Players use bluffing and deduction to discover secret objectives, telling convincing lies to cover up their true intentions and to gain trust from other players – all while avoiding death by zombies. Messy.

Campaign and legacy games

Legacy games allow players to permanently adapt and change their board with each play of the game. Every game builds on the events of the previous one and new rules, mechanisms, components and events are revealed during different plays. One of the best in this genre is **Pandemic Legacy**. This takes the popular co-operative game **Pandemic** to a new level as players work through a series of 12 games that represent the months of a year. You have two chances to achieve each month's objectives, so you have a maximum of 24 plays of the game. As with all legacy games, because you permanently alter the board, you can only play the full game once. If you like the idea of a game that progresses from play to play, but want more replayability, you should look for games with campaign modes. These give different starting and victory conditions as you play through the games. The modern classic **Catan** has a Seafarers expansion pack that adds a campaign mode to the game. In **Arkham Horror: The Card Game** you play through a series of adventures that impact upon the future landscape of the game. When you feel you've exhausted the published campaigns, you could delve into the huge number of fan-created scenarios available for download online.

Role-playing games (RPGs)

Create and develop your own character and then join others in an adventure. You'll immerse yourself in the game as you explore and expand your world, all the time using your character's skills and knowledge to develop the narrative. Most RPGs are set in the fantasy worlds of elves, orcs and goblins, but not all. *Good Society*, a Jane Austin inspired RPG, clearly has a different setting. The most well-known RPG is still *Dungeons and Dragons*, but – as in the wider world of board gaming – there is a surge of new RPGs and so a huge number to choose from. Try **Legacy of Dragonholt**, a narrative game in which you create your own unique hero and then embark on a noble quest. This game brilliantly captures the essence of RPGs without needing a gamemaster or extensive set-up.

GAMES THAT REVOLVE AROUND CARDS

Collectible card games (CCGs)

Vast numbers of new cards are released in sealed packs which players purchase in the hopes of getting some good cards. From the cards you acquire, you build your own deck to battle other people. Online auction sites are doing very nicely out of CCGs as players will, seemingly happily, spend a ton of money on acquiring a single card that will fit their deck. The two biggest CCGs are **Magic: The Gathering** and **Pokémon Trading Card**

Game. *Magic: The Gathering* has an enormous fan base. It is played all over the world – particularly on Friday nights when 'Friday Night Magic' groups can be found in basements and game shops in every corner of the planet. Most CCGs have a fantasy theme, and many have beautiful artwork. In *Magic: The Gathering*, for example, each creature, land, artefact, spell and planeswalker (some of the most powerful beings in the multiverse) is illustrated and three or four new sets are released each year.

Deck-building games

Starting with a small identical set of basic cards, players use cards from their hand to purchase more-advanced cards from the general supply and add them to their decks. At the start of each new turn, players draw cards from their deck to form their new hand. As the advanced cards come into play, players perform ever more powerful actions. The aim is to build a personal deck of cards that enables you to generate income, influence or points. Deck-building games allow you to reuse the cards you curate multiple times as you play through your deck before you shuffle and play through it again. In *Dominion*, as in many other deck-building games, players draw the top few cards from their deck each turn, then play the cards they have in their hand. Turns are taken rapidly. The same card choices are open to all players to purchase, but players' strategies will vary and with it their card selection. Each game of *Dominion* is different as players randomly select 10 of the 25 action cards in the box to play with. Bag-building games, such as *Altiplano*, have applied the deck-building system to tokens. These tokens are carefully selected by the players, purchased and then added to the player's own cloth bag. Tokens are drawn randomly from the bag at the start of each turn, influencing the actions available to the player. Players influence the element of luck by refining and developing their deck or bag.

Trick-taking and hand management games

Based on old, standard card games like Whist and Bridge, trick-taking games involve players selecting cards from their hand to play in order to win rounds and gain the advantage. Some use standard playing cards, but these days most new games are likely to have their own systems and sets of bespoke cards. Try *Nyet!*, in which players, taking on the role of Soviet-era anthropomorphised animal characters, influence the conditions of the round before playing each hand. *Diamonds* comes with two sets of very pleasing diamond components, which players aim to seize control of by winning tricks. Depending on the suit of the trick taken, players may take diamonds from a central supply, steal from another person or put them in their vault for safekeeping. Trick-taking games often have the advantage of being great 'fillers', in that you can play a few quick hands when you only have 20–30 minutes.

GAMES IN WHICH TIME MATTERS

Real-time games

Many games involve turn-by-turn actions, meaning that players take turns in order, one after another. Other games involve simultaneous play, meaning all players perform specific actions at the same time. In each of these cases, however, play can be paused to wait for players to make decisions. This is not the case for real-time games. Real-time games play out as fast as the players are able to play them. *Captain Sonar* is a game for up to 8 players, in which two teams each control a submarine. The captain of each team decides the route of their submarine and plots it on a map, communicating each movement loudly so that the radio operator on the rival team can hear and monitor. The engineer and the first mate on each team manage the vessel's internal systems and all players must communicate effectively to avoid detection while finding the exact location of the enemy submarine. Your submarine moves as quickly as your team can move it. Play is frantic and loud, but very great fun. This is not one for the faint-hearted.

Escape games

The aim of escape games (or exit games) is to provide a complete escape room experience in a box. Working co-operatively as a team, players tackle a series of puzzles as quickly as possible to try to complete the whole story within 60 minutes. No part of the box can be dispensed with in case a clue is hidden. Most escape games can only be played once, with many requiring you to destroy the components as you progress through the scenario. However, prices usually reflect this single-use play. If you fancy your chances, try *Exit the Game: The Abandoned Cabin*, but make sure that you've cleared a full hour, as even a quick trip to the toilet could waste valuable minutes and thwart your chances of escape.

Action and dexterity games

Players gain the advantage by flicking, spinning, removing, building or balancing components. A steady hand is a huge advantage in all these games, so this is one category in which the very young and the very old are unlikely to be able to compete on a level playing field. Dexterity games have come a long way since *Tiddlywinks* and *Pick Up Sticks*. In **Tokyo Highway**, the aim is to build roads over or under your opponents' roads and gain points as you do so. Players must carefully balance their roads on cylinders as they build. The resulting structure is a work of art. Make sure you take a photo before it all comes tumbling down. If you're looking for a less precise game in which a small knock of the table won't signal catastrophe, **PitchCar** will have you flicking disc-shaped 'cars' around a racetrack. The right mix of accuracy and power will see your car out in front. Many dexterity games also contain an element of speed.

GAMES BASED ON A MAP OR GRID

Action/movement programming games

Programming games allow you to secretly plan and 'lock in' your movements in advance. These games usually involve simultaneous action, requiring you to make your own decisions before you know how other players are going to move. In **Room 25**, players are trying to escape from a nightmare prison. But some players may actually be guards, whose secret objective is to prevent escape. As you program and lock in your moves, you must negotiate with other players and try to work out who to trust. When players reveal their actions, you may see the trap that you're going to fall into, but you are powerless to prevent it. You'll need to effectively balance potential risk with reward for the best chances of escape.

Area control and area movement games

Usually centred around a map, area control games require you to gain majority influence in one area of the board through the placement of your units, using manipulation or attack. Games that include area movement allow players to travel between connected geographical areas on the board. A classic area control and area movement game is **Risk**, in which players move their troops around the world to try to conquer the most territory. Area control games usually require players to keep a good overall view of the world to plan their expansion. In some games, once you have claimed an area, it is yours for the game. In **Five Tribes**, for example, on each turn you drop a trail of meeples which ends in the area that you wish to claim. You must plan your action in order to claim an area that will provide you with the best and most useful combinations of resources to ultimately help you win points. Whereas in other area control games, such as **Small World**, in which you'll control a series of fantasy races using your special powers, you have to plan how you will defend your regions to prevent them from being attacked, while gaining ground by threatening others' territory.

GAMES INVOLVING INDIRECT PLAYER INTERACTION

Tile placement games

Players construct the game board by laying tiles in ways that will help their own play while hindering their opponents. In **Carcassonne**, players construct a landscape of fields, roads, cities and monasteries. At each turn, players lay down one tile and decide whether or not to place one of their meeples on the tile to activate a feature. Players must plan the placement of their tiles and meeples to maximise the points they'll receive during the game. The tiles in **Carcassonne** are added to a communal playing area, but in other games – such as **Cottage Garden**, in which players place polyomino-shaped flower bed tiles into their own gardens, and **Azul** – players select tiles to create a personal tableau. **Azul**, a (largely) abstract game, requires players to draft tiles from the centre of the table, before placing them on their board to create patterns and complete sets.

Worker placement (or action drafting) games

A set of actions are available to all players, and each must select which ones to take on their turn. Actions will differ from game to game but may include drawing cards, claiming limited resources, purchasing goods or building structures. Because players cannot take every action, they must decide which are the most important or time-sensitive actions that they should prioritise. There may be a good deal of competition for some actions as players fight for food, money or some other in-game currency. A good example of a worker placement game is **Agricola**, in which players develop their farm by planting crops, building fences, raising animals, extending the farmhouse and purchasing upgrades. As the game progresses and the farms grow, ever more powerful actions will come into play. Before you decide to take all the wood so you can add an extension to your farmhouse, make sure you can feed your family, or the penalties will be steep.

COMBINING MECHANICS

Games will often combine multiple mechanics within a chosen theme. For example, **Mayfly** is a co-operative deck-building card game where the players try to keep a male mayfly alive. **Viticulture** is an economic worker placement and hand management game in which players take on the roles of people in rustic Tuscany who have inherited meagre vineyards. The possible combinations of mechanics and themes are endless.

There's lots I've not covered here, including: auction and bidding, memory, pick up and deliver, set collection, route/network-building, roll and write, storytelling and party games. The clue really is in the name in a lot of these instances, though examples of these will appear at various points throughout the rest of the book. There is good reason for this omission: as I mentioned, *Board Game Geek* counts 51 different types of game mechanics – we'd be here a long time going into each and every one – so I've tried to give a broad but not overwhelming overview. Keep experimenting with different types of games until you find a sweet spot for your family. Then experiment some more.

PODCASTS AND MAGAZINES

Listening to board-gaming podcasts is a great way to discover new games that the family might enjoy. To hook your children in and spark their interest, download a few podcast episodes and play them in the car, where you have a captive audience. I recommend starting with *The Dice Tower* – an American podcast that, at the time of writing, has recently released their six-hundredth episode, so there's quite a back catalogue to choose from.[2]

The Dice Tower reviews a huge range of games: new releases and shelf staples; quick fillers and weightier strategic epics; space races and dungeon crawlers. The presenters talk through games they've played recently, answer questions from listeners and create regular top ten lists for different types of games. If you've enjoyed **Yahtzee**, for instance, you can listen to them discuss their favourite roll and write games to delve a bit further into the genre.[3] In each case, a brief overview is given, which is enough to provide some ideas and encourage you to discover more.

For older teenagers and parents who don't mind a bit of swearing, try the *Tuesday Knight Podcast*, an entertaining and sometimes hilarious romp through games new and old.[4] Start with an episode number ending in a zero (e.g. 70 or 120) as these have been designed to help new listeners get a feel for the podcast, with a more thorough explanation of each of the subjects under discussion.

This passive exposure to the hobby may offer your first window onto what sorts of games appeal to your family. Listen out for positive noises and, without pushing, ask if they'd be interested in playing that game. This might instigate a speedy withdrawal into headphones, but you might get murmur of assent or even a surprisingly enthusiastic response.

Tabletop Gaming is a glossy magazine for the UK board-gaming community. Use it to find out about new games (and old games) of all varieties and to discover upcoming local events.[5]

Ultimately, the aim should be for your family to fully and enthusiastically embrace their status as a board game family. When that is the case, you may find each member of your family actively involved in researching and selecting new games. Until that time, increasing your family's exposure to

---

2 See https://www.dicetower.com/game-podcast/dice-tower.
3 See https://www.dicetower.com/news/tdt551-favorite-roll-and-writes.
4 See http://www.tuesdayknightgames.com/podcast.
5 See https://www.tabletopgaming.co.uk/.

up-to-date information about the hobby will not only broaden their interest, but give them reference points for discovering new information in the future. For example, listening to *The Dice Tower* podcast in the car might ultimately encourage them to look at their reviews online.

CHAPTER 4

MASTER THE METAGAME

Become a great player and teacher of the only game that matters.

THE METAGAME IS THE MOST IMPORTANT GAME

Playing the game on the table is only part of the overall experience. Even before the box is open, the metagame has begun. The metagame is the drama unfolding between the players. The metagame involves manipulating the emotions of your opponents. The metagame gives you the feeling of triumph that comes from collaborative problem-solving.

Have you ever won a board game but taken so little pleasure in it that you felt like you had lost? That's the metagame. Have you ever followed someone else's lead in a team game, against your better judgement, and been thrilled with their downfall? That's the metagame. Have you ever been so pleased by winning a battle that it made no difference that you lost the war? Yes, that's the metagame.

We have all played games that are just awful, but we've had an amazing time because the mood has been right and the group has been happy. Most of us would choose this over playing a brilliant game in a stormy atmosphere, heavy with sneers and sighs. The metagame holds such power over game-playing families that it is a much more important factor in their enjoyment than the actual game on the table is. The problem is that it is sometimes difficult to tell what metagame is being played until it is well underway.

As parents, we often try to influence the metagame by reminding the players to be nice to each other. However, just proclaiming that winning doesn't matter and that it is the taking part that counts doesn't make it true for the players. While the playing of the board game is contained within time and space, the metagame is much bigger. The metagame may not start with a level playing field. The son who has just convinced his parents that his sister is to blame for some household crime, while getting off scot-free himself, has far more metaphorical cash in his bank than his sister does in hers. The younger daughter who has just passed her driving test first time, while her elder sister waits to retake it (again), has a serene protective shield around her, making her immune to attack, despite her sister's best efforts.

It's not just general family life that impacts the metagame – events of previous game nights play their part as well. The memory of an important alliance severed in a moment of gleeful backstabbing might provoke a wary mistrust that sounds the death knell to tonight's co-operative game. Someone's (very lucky) win in a previous game may trigger a loud, cocky and wildly overconfident performance the next time the box is brought out, infuriating everyone else and ultimately making their messy demise all the more dramatic. So, if the metagame is so volatile, how do we tame and influence it?

It is difficult to set rules for the metagame. Setting rules would be like trying to control the emotions that people feel. If you've ever been told to calm down when you're in a rage, you'll understand that directing other people's emotions isn't that easy. So this isn't about establishing the rules and then trying to enforce them; it's about influence. Influencing your family while they play games will take a bit of thought, preparation and probably some practice. You may even have to significantly change your own behaviour to start to guide the behaviour of others.

Let me get one thing straight. There is nothing wrong with being competitive. In fact, game playing relies on it. There is nothing worse than playing a game with a group of players who aren't trying to win. Having the aim of winning develops strategies, sharpens problem-solving and improves the skills needed in order to achieve. People who don't try to win are just passengers, and winning against them doesn't feel like a win at all. We want to know that we've won on our own merit. Being *allowed* to win is only a triumph on the surface. But there is a big difference between *playing* to win and *needing* to win. The competitive parent *needs* to win and may exhibit some nasty metagaming tactics in order to do so. To become a master of the metagame you first need to take an honest look at your own behaviour. Deliberately and consistently model the behaviours you want to see. Try to retain your objectivity so that even while you are concentrating on the game on the table, you're always aware of the metagame.

HOW TO TEACH GAMES

After acquiring a new game, it's important to properly prepare its introduction to the family. It isn't always easy to get the whole family sitting down together at the table, and you don't want to waste precious game-playing time by being disorganised. Here are some 'rules' to help you to get everyone absorbed in new games quickly.

Rule 1: unbox well before you play

Unboxing a new game is one of the great delights of board gaming. Tearing off the cellophane, uncovering the shiny new components, popping counters out of pristine cardboard surrounds, un-bagging intriguing plastic resources, marvelling at cute wooden meeples and opening out the game board for the first time is an exciting experience. Some games take a lot of time to unbox. You may have to construct elements from scratch and there will undoubtedly be quite a lot of sorting. When you've cleared the pile of recycling that you've created, lay everything out on the table and check that you have all the components. Most rule books will list the components, usually with pictures, so you can check them off one by one. Work out what each individual component is and how it is referred to in the game rules. Getting familiar with the game lingo will help you to teach it to others. Feel free to unbox with the family as this is a ritual that can be very exciting, but don't be tempted to play immediately after unboxing unless you already know the rules really well. If the game is new to you, make it clear to the family that even though unboxing is taking place today, playing will be tomorrow. If there is the expectation that you are going to play immediately after unboxing, this stage will be rushed: pieces may go missing and you won't have time to prepare the game properly or learn how to play yourself.

Rule 2: learn how to play the game on your own

This is the most important rule. Unless you regularly play hundreds of games and are really familiar with game mechanics, it is almost impossible to read and understand a rule book when under pressure from a table of expectant players. Some rule books are badly written, confusing and long-winded. Even concise and brilliantly crafted rules need to be read and understood before you can communicate the game clearly to others. There is nothing more frustrating than watching someone read the rules for 20 minutes before you can play. It is hard to stay quiet and invariably this leads the rule-reader to distraction. Not a good way to start a game night. If you've not had time to learn the new game beforehand, play a different one.

Once on your own, lay all the pieces out on the table and open the rule book. Set the game up for the player count you are most likely to have the first time you play. I find that the easiest way to learn the game play is to watch a how-to-play video on YouTube. There are multiple videos for every possible game. When you have a good overview, you might then look back at the rule book to consider the structure of the rounds or the actions you can select. It is sometimes useful to watch longer videos of full games being played out, particularly of those with more complicated rules or lots of components. This gives you a really good feel for the flow of the game. Now you should start to play a few rounds on your own, taking all the turns yourself. The aim is to become so familiar with the game that when you are teaching it to others, you aren't constantly having to remind yourself of the rules, structure and actions.

Rule 3: plan how you are going to teach the game

The slicker the teaching of the game, the better. When you are watching how-to-play videos, take some time to notice how the presenters are teaching. It is usually a good idea to start with the aim of the game and the victory conditions. For some games, you might also need to give a quick thematic overview – explaining the context and setting. Don't get caught up in reading out sections from the rule book, because it will contain far more information than the family needs to start playing. Work out what everyone needs to know to be able to start the game and plan to tell them this. Explain turn structure and some of the basic actions. It is absolutely fine to start playing a game without all the information being given upfront. Write yourself a mini teaching plan, with reminders about what elements you're going to share before you get started.

Try to limit your initial introduction to ten minutes. Within ten minutes you should be playing, either having launched into the game proper, or playing a few practice rounds to experience the game in action. You should take time to consider the specific needs of your family. If there are adults or children with attention issues, make sure you dive quickly into the game and learn through playing. Avoid lengthy explanations and plan to reveal additional information during play. If you have any players with autistic spectrum disorders, they may wish to understand all the rules before beginning. In this case, you might want to spend some time with this individual, teaching them the game more fully or allowing them to read from the rule book prior to playing with the family. Whatever the needs of your family, avoid jumping in with no thought or planning. Your masterful preparation can have a huge impact on the success of the game and on how often the family will want to play it in the future.

Rule 4: don't take it personally

Learning how to teach games can be pretty difficult. It is a skill that game designers, developers, demonstrators and industry experts have practised and honed over time – and not all of them are good at it. It is unlikely that every explanation you give will be immediately understood. You might launch into a game and then bear the brunt of anger when players claim that you haven't communicated a rule properly or that they would have made a different decision if they had understood. You won't get any thanks for a brilliantly crafted explanation that helps everyone play without issue, but you'll certainly get it in the neck when things go wrong. That is just the way it is. It is the same for any teacher, but it is even more likely you'll be on the receiving end of abuse when playing with your own family. Don't take it personally.

Unless the rules are *very* simple, playing a game for the first time can be hard. There may be multiple ways to play and even multiple ways to win. As a player, you're forced to make decisions from the first turn, without understanding their full impact. But it's like that for everyone. Find a way to communicate this to your family. If everyone understands that it will take them a few plays to get used to the mechanisms and to experiment with tactics, they are less likely to get stressed on the first try. You might have a rule about not totalling scores until you've played twice, for example, as this will take the pressure off and reduce the chances of the game teacher being in the firing line.

Rule 5: draw on other resources to teach the game

If you found a game easy to learn from a five-minute YouTube video, share that video with the family as an introduction. If you learned a game from a friend, ask the friend to come over and teach your family. Having an external person as the teacher can really help to reduce conflict the first time you play. Or you could teach in conjunction with another member of the family, so that there are two people who already know how to play the game and can answer questions or conduct demonstration rounds. Another alternative is to teach everyone in smaller groups, enabling you to tailor your explanation to individuals within the family.

Rule 6: you don't need to teach strategy

Good games feature layers of strategy and, when you know about these, there is a temptation to teach new players how to strategise. But part of the fun of playing new games is working out the puzzle for yourself, forming your own connections, making your own discoveries and testing your own ideas. Making strategic decisions is rewarding and interesting. Most players would prefer to lose on their own than win with someone else's ideas. Whether you win or lose, you remember the tactical decisions you made and use these as a basis to work from the next time you play.

The exception to this rule is around the extremes. If there is a particularly powerful strategy, you may like to draw attention to it. If there is a major pitfall to be avoided in the game, let the players know upfront. In some cases, it is a good idea to show players specific cards that might come up during the game, so that they understand some of the implications. Whenever you do give strategy advice - even if it is very broad - make sure you offer it to the whole group, rather than focusing your help on individuals, unless this has been specifically requested. Stop yourself jumping in when you see players making questionable decisions and let them work it out for themselves. They might just come up with a winning strategy that hasn't crossed your mind.

Rule 7: treat all players equally

Don't underestimate the strategic brainpower of a 9-year-old. Unless you are playing super-complicated games in which some players might need assistance to keep all the rules and conditions clear in their mind, younger and older players should be given the same initial support and instruction. Most light strategy games enable players of different ages to compete on a level playing field. A child doesn't need to be able to see all the possible strategies in order to find an effective one. A player doesn't need to be able to identify all the possible implications of their decision in order to make a choice.

CHOOSING A GAME

The metagame starts well before the game does. Round 1 is deciding what game to play and getting it onto the table. This can be particularly difficult if individual players are fixated on one game or game type that the rest of the family don't enjoy. When family members have very different tastes in games, keeping everyone happy can be a challenge. Here are some different ways to decide what to play:

■ **Take it in turns.** The game-chooser role rotates around the family and you keep track of whose turn it is. Everyone plays the chosen game.

  🎲 Pros: Everyone gets to play the game they want to at regular intervals.

  🎲 Cons: There is a possibility that the majority will sit down to a game that they have no desire to play and bring all their huffiness and resentment with them.

  🎲 The verdict: Unless the family all have very similar tastes and you only own games that everyone enjoys, this route should be avoided as it could mean that, too much of the time, people are playing games they don't really want to play. This could be the death of family game night.

■ **Games in a hat.** Each player chooses the game that they'd prefer to play, writes the name on a piece of paper and puts it in a hat. One name is drawn. Everyone plays the randomly chosen game.

- Pros: This creates a game out of choosing, which most people enjoy, and which softens the blow if your game isn't chosen. Players accept that there is a fair chance their game will be played.

- Cons: One player may end up putting the same game in the hat each time and getting more and more cross when it isn't randomly selected.

- The verdict: This only works if everyone is in the right mood. If there are no time pressures and everyone is relaxed, it can be fun. Use on a long rainy Sunday or on the fifth day of a family holiday.

Random selection. Every game you own is written on a piece of paper and each is placed in a sparkly envelope, to increase the excitement of the draw. Different game lengths or player counts can be marked in code on the envelopes. Envelopes are placed in a box or barrel and one is chosen at random. That game is played. (Of course, you could just fold the pieces of paper up and mark the symbols on the back if you are a bit low on craft supplies.)

- Pros: Nobody controls the decision-making process. Power-play is avoided. You get to play games that you might not otherwise choose.

- Cons: You might end up with a game that several people really don't want to play.

- The verdict: If everyone is happy to play any game, this works well. Otherwise, this should be avoided as you could end up with a game that nobody wants to play.

Negotiated set of games. Together the family chooses a selection of games that everyone would be happy to play. The selected games have to be given the okay by each person to make it into the set. Then one game is chosen from the set at random. This is the game that is played.

- Pros: Everyone will definitely get to play a game they are happy with.

- Cons: It might take a while to negotiate the set. You may not have many games in the final set.

- The verdict: The set of agreed games may be small, and they may be of a very similar type. This isn't the best way to get variety, but it is a good option for peace-keeping, *if* you can agree a set in the first place.

One cuts, the other chooses. One person chooses a longlist of games they want to play, another person cuts down the selection, then another chooses the game from the shortlist. You can adjust the number of games the first person starts with and the number the set is cut by according to the size of your family – so, for example, with three people, the first person can choose five, the second cuts to three and the third selects from the three.

- Pros: Everyone has the opportunity to contribute to the decision. Each person can avoid playing games they really don't like.
- Cons: It can be a little hard to keep track of whose turn it is to do which stage.
- The verdict: This is my family's go-to method. Game selection hardly ever causes problems and each person is making a decision that is fairly quick and easy.

- **Games on rotation.** Keep a master list of all the board and card games the family has. Play the games on the list in rotation.

  - Pros: You play a wide variety of games so you won't get bored with playing the same games time and time again. Children who really like structure might respond well to the certainty of the rotation. Nobody has got the upper hand by getting their own way.
  - Cons: A situation in which nobody wants to play the scheduled game can arise frequently, and it may be a long time until you get to play your family favourites.
  - The verdict: This might work for game groups in which the metagame isn't so volatile, but this really isn't a viable solution for most families. It can, however, work brilliantly as a secondary game selection method, when used in conjunction with other methods.

- **Choose the game, then choose the players.** Someone proclaims, 'Oh, I fancy playing *Dice City*. Who wants to join me?' Players join in only if they want to.

  - Pros: Only players who want to play the game end up playing.
  - Cons: There may be some members of the family who end up not taking part because they don't like that game, even though they'd like to play with everyone.
  - The verdict: Excellent for ad hoc gaming, but not so great if everyone knows it is the dedicated game night and a controversial title is chosen.

- **Loser chooses.** The player who lost the previous game chooses the next one. Everyone plays whatever this player wants to play.

  - Pros: Acts as a sweetener for the loser.

- Cons: Players might deliberately throw a game so they can choose the next. There is a lack of negotiation and choice for most players, which can put backs up. It is hard to keep track of who lost last time.

- The verdict: Unless you are playing a string of games on one day, the advantage of choosing next time is pretty minimal. Delayed gratification is never that appealing, particularly to young children. This method is unsatisfactory and causes more problems than it solves.

- **Group decision prior to playing.** At the end of one game night, the group decides together which games are going to be played next time. The decision is recorded and the games are played without question.

  - Pros: Everyone is involved in the decision-making process. The family can prepare for the next game night. Everyone knows what is coming to the table and can get excited about it.

  - Cons: Some players may have changed their minds and might not actually feel like playing the agreed games.

  - The verdict: This is great for big, involved games that require several hours of playing time. It is also a good option when planning a game night with several lighter games. It reduces the time spent on decision-making and gets everyone onto game playing straight away.

- **Path of least resistance.** Games are suggested to the family until it becomes clear which one will sit reasonably comfortably with most people. The game that seems like the best compromise is played.

  - Pros: You get as many people to play as possible.

  - Cons: The negotiation and decision-making phase may take quite a lot of time.

  - The verdict: This is the standard process for many families and seems to work well if the atmosphere is a little strained. Ultimately, the parent holds the negotiations and makes the decision about the game that is played, so any issues that arise are directed towards them.

Jumping into conflict-avoidance mode at the sign of the smallest unrest is a normal state of affairs for many wary parents. But if members of your family are successful in getting their own way through emotional manipulation, then they will continue to do so. The daughter who kicks off when the game she wants to play is out-voted, only to see her response resulting in the family backing down, will continue to kick off to get the same result. If a game is selected that someone doesn't want to play, they don't have to play. So, despite the hairdryer treatment she's directing at the family, it's best to tell your screaming daughter that she can sit this one out. Continue without her or give her five minutes to calm down and slink back to the table.

The parent's role here isn't as peacekeeper. Rather you should see yourself as the teacher of gamesmanship. Family members who are used to getting their own way when selecting games will carry this behaviour into the game itself (and into other aspects of family life). The teacher of gamesmanship aims to turn bad losers into good losers, bad winners into good winners and players who freak out when they don't get their own way into players who accept disappointment humbly and calmly. Well, that is the *aim*.

The teacher of gamesmanship will use all the game selection methods that I've listed in different situations. They'll see the game selection very much as the first round in the metagame, and as an opportunity to train and test the players. When games are predictable, they become dull, and the players may develop strategies to cheat or exploit the weaknesses of the system. If the selection method is constantly changing, there is no opportunity for boredom and subterfuge. The teacher of gamesmanship takes care not to favour one player over another. In turn, the players develop trust in this impartiality, taking setbacks more gallantly and good-naturedly.

OFFERING ADVICE AND HELP

Once the game is underway and you've played through a couple of turns, it may be that one player is taking an early lead or has suffered an early setback. Games in which the eventual winner or loser is clear after the first round or so are rare (and probably pretty badly designed). It is normal to compare your position with others as you go through the game, but it can be a negative distraction for some players. If one of your opponents is making a big deal of their advances as you are suffering a false start, that frustration is heightened. Now is the time for gentle reinforcement of good gamesmanship.

Remind players who are boasting or lauding their brilliance over others about the importance of humility and kindness. To the ones lagging behind, emphasise the value of a positive outlook. Instead of wallowing in self-pity, the underdog can quietly calculate how to make a brilliant and unexpected comeback. Try to develop a series of non-verbal cues to remind your family about the sort of behaviour you expect to see. If these go unnoticed or ignored, take the transgressor outside the room for a very brief reminder.

This isn't about admonishment; it's a really gentle reminder of the impact of their behaviour on themselves and the others around the table. Set out your expectations clearly and remind them of their previous brilliant behaviour. Do so quickly and get back to the game. Crucially, make sure you notice when your family behave in the way you want them to. If they only get your attention for behaving in the wrong way, they won't change. Take the time to tell them how impressed you are when they react modestly to successes or with gumption to setbacks.

At times, particularly when playing from the back of the field, your children may get themselves tied in knots and find it difficult to see how to make a good decision about their game play. This could leave them frozen in a haze of indecision, or fighting back tears of frustration. We want our children to make their own decisions, but we also want to be able to help and support them to make the best decisions possible. Unfortunately, children don't always want to accept their parents' help.

It is a common lament from parents that their kids just won't accept their efforts to teach them. If helping your son with a maths problem or teaching your daughter how to serve in tennis has ever ended in a messy explosion of temper, you will know what I'm talking about. If teenagers were happy to learn from their parents, then all driving instructors would be out of a job. So, what is the problem? Why is it so hard for parents to formally teach their children? Well, the relationship is complicated, much more complicated than a student–teacher relationship. The teaching is mixed up with emotions, expectations, past experiences and judgements. To teach effectively, you must remain objective and calm. That is pretty hard for parents. Also, the 'student' has to be receptive to the learning. Many parents try to teach when their help hasn't actually been asked for. Children may not want to ask for help. Asking for help isn't easy, particularly in front of other members of the family. Many people would rather fail on their own than succeed with help from others. This may sound crazy, but there it is. Children want to impress their parents. They don't want to show weakness or a lack of understanding.

So, what should we do when our children struggle with a board game? It may be clear to us that they need help or advice, or even just a reminder of the rules, but how can we manipulate the metagame to enable them to feel comfortable and in control?

- Don't give advice or help until you are asked. Offer help if you wish, but don't insist on giving it if your offer is rejected.

- Avoid deconstructing players' decisions after the fact. Informing your children about what they could have done during the game and why that would have worked better is not helpful.

- Allow your children to make their own decisions. Even if they've asked for advice, don't insist that they follow it.

- Give your advice lightly. Emphasise that your opinion is just one opinion.

- Make it clear that the decision is not an easy one and that there are lots of possible options that may lead to equally good outcomes.

- Play down your expertise. Assure your child that you possess no special skills that will make your thinking any more worthy than their own.

- Boost your child's belief in their own ability. Remind them of times in previous games when they've made great decisions or triumphed in difficult circumstances.

- Give opportunities for children to save face. Preface sentences with, 'I'm sure you've worked this out already …' or 'Well, you will already know this but …'

- Reinforce the equal nature of your positions. Demonstrate your own status as a learner of the game, ask your children for help with your own game play and take their advice, whether you need it or not.

- Whatever decision is ultimately taken, be clear that you support and understand that decision and that you think they are making a decent choice.

There is, of course, another issue at play here. We are not only asking our children to accept our advice as a parent, but as a competitor. A competitor who, according to the rules of the game, will ultimately only triumph if they play better than their children. It is easy to tailor your advice to create the best outcome for yourself as a player. Be warned, this will be sniffed out quickly by your children and that may be the last time they ask for your help. There is a fine balance of trust here. You need to retain complete objectivity. It is useful to think about what you would advise if you weren't playing the game yourself. Put your cards down, move away from your space, take your metaphorical game-playing hat off and position yourself alongside your child. If their hidden cards are revealed to you, you'll have to forget them, or play as if you don't know what they are. Your assurances that you can help without benefitting your own game will only be believed if your subsequent actions support this.

MANAGING DOWNTIME

Most games require players to take turns individually. While other players are taking their turns, you are waiting. This is *downtime*.

Downtime has its benefits. You have time to plan ahead and to assess the field. You can work through different scenarios in your mind, weighing up the associated benefits and drawbacks. You can also watch other players, examine their choices, aim to discover their objectives and learn from their tactics. Or you may prefer to chat to other players about the game (or about other things). But downtime can also have frustrations, particularly for less-patient players and especially for anyone with attention issues.

To keep everyone actively engaged in the game, it is useful to minimise downtime, without cutting thinking time too drastically. Each game will require different amounts of turn time and thinking time, dependent on the number and complexity of the actions taken each go. So what works for one game may not work for another. Resist the desire to leave the table to put the kettle on or to fetch a batch of biscuits when waiting for someone else to play. Your behaviour is a model for everyone else's. If you leave the table, you are setting a precedent. Remember, you are playing games so that you can all be together, at the table, engaged in the same activity. Experiment with ideas to manage downtime in different games to maintain everyone's interest. Here are some things you could try:

- **Incorporate planning time.** Add house rules to allow players to plan their next move *while* others are taking their turns. For example, adapt *Carcassonne*, the wonderful tile placement game, by picking up your next tile at the end of your previous turn, rather than at the start of your new turn. This allows you lots of thinking time while other players are playing and helps to speed up the game. This thinking time is written into other games like *Dominion* and *Dice City*, in which the last thing you do on your turn is prepare for the next.

- **Use timers to limit turn time.** Make sure the time allowed works for the game: this may require some experimentation and discussion. Introduce the timer before you start the game and get the agreement of all players. Remind them that sometimes they'll run out of time and have to make snap decisions, but this will be the same for everyone. Or purchase a DGT Cube - a six-sided game timer which means each player has their own clock with which to keep track of their time. Different turn lengths can be set for different players, helping to differentiate for younger or less-experienced players.

Reduce distractions. Try to get an agreement about no phones at the table or at least put phones on silent. Looking at your phone when it isn't your turn divides your attention and slows the game down. It is harder to snap back into the game if you are distracted by online chat.

Establish a sub-game. If you have a lot of game components, create your own dexterity game with players aiming to make interesting towers of meeples and resource cubes. Adding a small tabletop sideshow won't distract from the main game and will keep everyone at the table. Or play hot-word: a game in which each player secretly makes a list of five phrases that they expect their opponents to utter at some point. When the phrase is spoken, it is crossed off. The first player to cross off all their hot-words wins this sub-game.

Give roles to each player. Different members of the family can take responsibility for different game components and elements. You could be the chief shuffler, banker, scorekeeper or resource manager. Each role could be represented by a badge, an appropriate item of costume – for example, a bowler hat for the banker to wear when handling money – or a catchphrase. These roles increase engagement, as players will often be required to perform their tasks during other people's turns, but the division of tasks also can speed up the game.

Assign game-support roles to players. These jobs do not affect the game play, but do provide a game-related focus in moments of downtime. The official photographer can document the game, creating a dramatic photostory of the game night. The house reporter can chronicle the game play, tracking the highlights and disasters in the game journal or recording audio for the family gaming blog (more about this in Chapter 7). The tabletop review hero can compile a list of the pros and cons of the game, analysing the mechanics and interviewing other players about their views. The artist in residence can create a masterpiece depicting the world of the game and the action unfolding within it.

Add narration and/or storytelling. Set the expectation that each player talks through their moves on their turn. Just watching players silently moving a few pieces can be pretty dull, but when players share their thought process and explain what they are doing it keeps others much more engaged, opens the door to negotiation and enables the family to learn from each other. Give your meeples names, personalities and a backstory. Explain the characters' motivations behind moves and decision-making.

If members of your family are very easily bored, choose games in which turns are very quick, like the deck-building game **Dominion**, or the spice-trading game **Century Spice Road**, for example, or play simultaneous action selection or real-time games, such as **Telestrations**, **Cash 'n Guns**, **7 Wonders** or *Exit the Game* escape room games. In these, everyone is playing all the time and downtime is greatly reduced or, in some cases, eliminated.

As the teacher of gamesmanship, you must stay alert even when it isn't your turn, because it's vital that you recognise the triumphs of the family. If another player performs a particularly clever combination of moves or manages to set up some board-gaming wizardry over a number of turns, make sure you notice this and comment on it. Your warm and genuine praise is the lifeblood of the metagame. Your ability to step outside your own play and take the time to observe, encourage and commend, even when you are the victim of your children's cunning tactics, models true gamesmanship and sets an important precedent. If you're clearly not watching, your children won't try as hard to impress you. When you switch off, they may switch off too.

EMBRACING TENSION

Some games accelerate as they progress, eventually going at breakneck speed before someone wins and the game stops with a jolt. This is particularly true of engine-building games. Here 'engine' refers to a player's accumulated cards or resources, rather than the mechanical construction of an actual engine. An engine builder warms up slowly, often taking many turns to gather a few resources. Cards are acquired that have no immediate benefit but that may help later on. Victory points start off being very hard to come by, but at some point it is like a switch is flicked and then, at each turn, certain cards help to maximise the potential of others. Many engine-building games allow players to form sequences of actions, where one action triggers another and another and another. Players are rewarded for the time they've spent in developing their engines so the component parts work well together.

In a recent two-player game of **Terraforming Mars**, my son Alfie had been leading almost from the start of the game. Some early decisions helped to generate points that kept him a good way ahead. But then the strategy I'd been working on since the start of the game started to pay off. Cards that increased my titanium production started to take effect, which allowed me to build high-value space cards every turn – my engine kicked in. In one turn I caught up and (with a masterful Giant Ice Asteroid and Water Import from Europa combo), I swiped the last available victory points, prevented my incredulous son from performing his carefully planned game-winning move and won by a single point. Fortunately, having undergone many years of intensive gamesmanship training, he took the defeat fairly well, though was clearly pretty shocked. (As a side note, I'm sure Alfie would like me to mention that he usually wins **Terraforming Mars**.)

As the race goes up a gear, so the emotions around the table can rise. Turn order, which previously felt like a formality, suddenly becomes absolutely critical. Rapid calculations are made, and moves planned, as players try to predict what others are about to do. As players' resource engines are on view for all to see, the player who has previously been concentrating only on their own game plan may suddenly look up and realise that an opponent is about to take the win and there is now nothing they can do about it. In **Splendor**, players gather cards representing different jewels. Just *owning* these jewels, which are all displayed on the table, allows players to acquire further jewel cards of ever-increasing value. The jewels that are available for acquisition are displayed and replenished whenever one is taken. The winner is the first player to gather 15 points. At some point, players may have accumulated enough jewels to acquire cards that give them 4 or 5 points each turn. The end of the game then follows rapidly, often much more rapidly than players are expecting. While all players' jewels are on display for the whole game, it is easy to solely focus on your own jewel-engine and forget to keep an eye on everyone else's. The tension during the last few turns is palpable as each player tries to claim the most points while preventing opponents from taking game-winning cards.

Good board games have mechanisms for growing tension built in. Tension largely comes from uncertainty. Uncertainty can occur through a variety of different mechanisms, including randomness, conflict with other players, restricted choices, hidden information or limited resources, actions or time. This tension is critical for engagement. Tension can turn a fun game into an all-consuming unforgettable experience that stays in your mind long after the game is packed away. Tension is the hook, the addictive element that will have the family returning to the table time and time again. Tension helps us to *care* about playing a game. Therefore, to make board gaming part of normal family life, we must embrace games that build tension, rather than trying to avoid them.

When the writing is on the wall, the tension suddenly disappears and the proverbial mess can hit the fan. Up until this moment, there is still everything to play for. Even if you have been playing catch-up for half the game, you've still had a chance. As soon as it becomes clear that there is no way that one player can be caught, or that another's position at the bottom of the pile is well and truly guaranteed, many people just want to throw in the towel. It is remarkable how many family games finish just minutes before the actual end of the game. It is hard for the losing player to complete the final turns, so much so that it might be preferable to walk away. But this abandonment isn't good gamesmanship. If the tables were turned, this family member would want to play out their carefully constructed winning moves and claim the victory. Denying someone else the chance to properly complete a game isn't fair. So, at the game's climax, the teacher of gamesmanship's main objective should be to keep all the players at the table, praising the defeated for continuing to participate with good cheer.

MANAGING CHEATING

Cheating is widespread in many families ... and it's not always the children. There are lots of different reasons why people might cheat. Some just feel the *need* to win: to reinforce their position within the family or because they feel that winning gives them importance. Some may blatantly and unashamedly cheat to provoke a reaction or to throw the game, particularly if they know they aren't going to win by playing fairly. Others may cheat because they attach no moral problem to cheating or because they feel that everyone else is cheating. If cheating is common, then this is perceived as expected and accepted behaviour. In some cases, cheating occurs due to underperformance worries: the player may want to win to bolster their self-confidence.

An unlucky roll of the dice, which causes a player to just miss out on a reward, may make them feel justified in making 'small adjustments'. The surreptitious re-roll of a dice, nudging a token along the board, pilfering from the bank or glancing at other people's cards are all forms of cheating. The outcome of the game isn't supposed to matter. It should be fun for everyone to play, whatever the result. So, if you are afflicted with dishonesty on game night, how can you reduce cheating and reinforce the idea that you should *play* to win but not *need* to win?

- Don't leave one person to do all the set-up on their own. Reduce the opportunity for cards to be ordered and resources to be manipulated before the game starts.

- Make it harder for players to cheat during the game. Place pooled resources and banks well away from individual players' boards, ideally slightly higher up (maybe on top of the box) and in full view of all players.

- If you suspect cheating during a game, pause and take a few moments to review the rules. Make sure it is really clear what qualifies as cheating and what behaviours and moves are acceptable.

- Avoid playing games that use mechanisms like rolling dice behind a screen as these rely on honesty and manipulating the outcome is too tempting for some.

- Make sure that there is no extrinsic motivation for winning. Neutralise the reasons why they might want to win as far as possible. Make sure you're praising brilliant play of the metagame and clever moves, rather than only rewarding the winner.

- Take time to talk to the culprit individually away from the game, possibly afterwards or even on another day. Avoid using the term 'cheating', but ask them why they felt the need to manipulate the results. Find ways to remind them about good gamesmanship and make sure you recognise their excellent choices in the next game.

- If necessary, declare the game void because you've noticed cheating. Don't openly state who you think the offender is, but remember to follow up later on. Then move briskly on to a different game.

The aim is to stop cheating while avoiding conflict. If openly challenged, most players will strongly deny that they've been cheating, even when caught red-handed. This just triggers confrontation, which is likely to cause more issues than it solves. As the metagame kicks in and the family learns that it is the way you play the game, rather than the outcome, which is important, cheating will reduce.

THE 'GET OUT'

Sometimes, despite our best intentions and preparations, things might not go according to plan. Board games should be fun and when someone stops having fun, they should be allowed to leave the table. However, when a player leaves a game before the end, it can be disruptive and may force everyone else to stop playing as well. Having some strategies for managing departing players helps to minimise the trouble it causes and prevents players who aren't having fun being strong-armed into finishing the game (which is never pretty). Next time you are unexpectedly a player down mid-game, try one of the following ideas. The strategy you choose will depend on the mechanics of the game you're playing:

- **Create a dummy hand.** Reveal the player's cards/resources/currency and keep them on display. This becomes the dummy hand. Players are able to trade with the dummy as they would with another player. The dummy may take part in any pure luck-based activity – for example, withdrawing resources from a bag, rolling dice, flipping cards – but should not take part in any activity that requires speed, dexterity, memory or decision-making. Except in luck-only games, the dummy is a partial player and could not win the game. Playing a dummy hand is the best solution to losing a player in games like *7 Wonders*. In this case, the cards would be chosen randomly for the dummy hand.

  Avoid this approach with games in which clever trading with opponents is a vital part.

- **Remove from play.** Clear the board of all pieces belonging to the departed player and remove them from the game completely. Play continues with the remaining players. This works for games like the deck builder *Dominion*, which contains many resources of the same type.

  Avoid this if resources are in short supply, if resources get recycled and reused or if the game is dependent on having certain components in active play.

- **Return to the bank.** Clear the board of all pieces belonging to the departed player and return the pieces to the bank. This enables other players to acquire them later in the game through normal game play. This is a good option for tile placement games like *Azul* and *Cottage Garden*, in which tiles are reused after being scored.

  Avoid this with games that end when resources run out.

- **Freeze the player.** Keep the departing player's pieces on the board. They are not allocated new resources and they do not take turns, but their pieces remain frozen. This works well with area control games like *Small World*, in which you can put the departing player's pieces into decline and treat them like 'lost tribes', and *Risk*, in which the departing player's armies become neutral. Both of these games have these mechanisms built into the starting conditions. Freezing a player in *Catan*, another area control game, prevents one player having an unfair advantage over others through their proximity to newly available resources.

Avoid this with games that are dependent on fair interactions between all players.

- **Distribute resources randomly.** Shuffle the cards/resources/currency and deal them out at random to the remaining players, who immediately add these to their own hoard. This is in keeping with the theme of the gangster-inspired *Cash 'n Guns*, in which players compete for a share of the loot – when one player dies, the others can rifle through his pockets. This is also the case in *Munchkin*, in which sharing the treasure of players who die is part of the game.

Avoid this with heavily strategic games in which there is little or no element of luck.

- **Distribute resources evenly.** Look at all the resources available and share them out evenly among the remaining players. If it is not possible to do this and there are resources left over, these can be removed from play or returned to the bank. This can be done in games like *Havana*, in which resources may be in short supply towards the end of the game, though it might speed up the end of the game as some buildings could become instantly available for purchase.

Avoid this with games in which there is a limit to the number of resources players may hold.

- **Hold an auction.** Reveal all of the departing player's resources. You can hold a quick viewing to allow each player to take a closer look (this might be necessary with some card games). Then auction off the resources in ascending order of value. Players bid for resources using their in-game currency. This works well in games like *Acquire*, which is based in the world of economic mergers and acquisitions.

Avoid this if the game currency is weak and much easier to come by than victory points.

- **Pool the resources.** The departing player's resources are placed on the table in full view of all players. These resources become freely available for any player to use any turn, rather than being traded in. There aren't many games in which this mechanism works, but it can give a twist to a classic like *Scrabble*, as players are suddenly able to construct words using additional tiles on top of the ones they have in play.

Avoid this with games that require components to be placed on an individual tableau to connect with other personal resources.

■ **Play face up.** The remaining players play the departing player's turns face up for all to see. Decisions are made collaboratively. This works with co-operative games like **Pandemic** and one-versus-many games like **Scotland Yard** (providing that the departing player wasn't playing Mr X, who the rest of the group is tracking). These games rely on negotiation and group decision-making, so playing one character face up often has very little impact on the overall game play.

Avoid this with games that rely on all players keeping information secret.

WINNERS AND LOSERS

Nowhere is the metagame more crucial than at the end of play. The winners and losers may be immediately obvious, or scores may need to be totted up to determine the standings. Either way, the point at which the winner is declared is a critical moment for the demonstration of good or bad gamesmanship.

Bad winners and bad losers display a range of behaviours, all powerful enough to ruin the experience for others. Good winners and good losers deal with the same situation in a different way. Here are some examples of poor conduct and how players possessing good gamesmanship might behave.

Bad winner	Good winner
Offers loud shouts of 'Yes! Yes!' while standing on a chair, swinging hips around, shooting imaginary guns into the air and laughing like a maniac.	Offers a kind smile and a gentle comment about being really pleased to have won and about how unexpected it was.

Bad winner	Good winner
Provides lengthy explanations of the successful strategy and tactics, possibly demonstrated by a full-blown reconstruction, with accompanying PowerPoint presentation.	Acknowledges the part that luck played in the victory and in others' less successful outcomes.
Immediately adopts the mantle of the expert to perform attacks on other people's game play from a position of assumed authority, followed by step-by-step instructions of how they should have played.	Shows interest in other people's strategies and begins positive discussions about individual tactics. Steers the conversation away from their own game play.
Aims pointing, jeering and general derision at the losing players. Makes sweeping comments about being a board game god and how the minions should bow and grovel.	Shows humility.
Refuses to pack up the game, claiming that their victory provides immunity from this dull task.	Offers to pack the game away so that others can leave the table.

Bad loser	Good loser
Bursts into a highly dramatic and very tearful tantrum, resulting in tear-stained playing cards and a snot-streaked board.	Makes a comment about being really disappointed and having hoped to be more successful.

Bad loser	Good loser
Directs hot-blooded anger at the game, the other players, the dice, the weather and the casserole eaten at lunch.	Accepts personal responsibility and acknowledges that some of their decisions could have been better.
Makes bitter accusations about cheating and assertions that the winner must have won through foul play.	Gives warm congratulations to the winner, accompanied by a pat on the shoulder or a formal handshake.
Flips the board before storming out and slamming the door, leaving the other players in a cloud of paper money with meeples bouncing on the floor.	Offers to pack the game away so that others can leave the table.
Makes bold declarations about never playing this game ever, ever again and banning others from even uttering its name in future.	Asks for advice from other players about tactics and strategy so that next time the game comes to the table, they can play differently.

I realise that the good winner and good loser columns may look like they describe some mythical model of perfect gamesmanship and, of course, it would be really weird if every player managed to tick all these boxes every time. Rather, bad and good behaviour exist on a spectrum. The good behaviour examples are what we can encourage the family to work towards. As teachers of gamesmanship, we should also be trying to model this ourselves whenever possible. It is very challenging to be a good loser when confronted with a bad winner. Even the most level and objective adult might struggle to remain calm in the face of outrageous ridicule from an overenthusiastic champion, but that is the *aim*.

When family members who have previously fallen well short of appropriate behaviour make improvements, it is critical to notice and to let them know that you've noticed. A child who is holding back the tears may be some way off making a rational comment about their disappointment, but is making a concerted attempt to avoid messily exploding. Recognition of their internal struggle and self-restrain by an adult will make the effort worthwhile. In time, your carefully chosen words will start to disrupt the child's habitual reactions and challenge the 'I need to win' mantra.

After the game is packed away, if appropriate, you may like to crown a winner of the metagame. The title should go to the player who has demonstrated the best gamesmanship. Instead of recording the scores, use a special notebook to write down important moments of excellent gamesmanship. Document metagame successes, so that you have evidence to refer back to in the future. As the family metagame book is gradually filled with accounts of outstanding behaviour, the way the players view themselves starts to change. Being a good loser and a good winner becomes the new normal. You know you've really cracked this when friends come over and your children are visibly shocked by their un-gamesmanly reactions.

GREAT GAMESMANSHIP TEACHES GREAT LIFEMANSHIP

When the metagame is well established and everyone's behaviours exhibit great gamesmanship, you will find your family's board gaming personas influencing other areas of family life. There are obvious parallels with sports - cheering for others, congratulating opponents, winning graciously and supporting your team - but this is not the limit of the impact. Board games enable players to become well-practised in failure. If you play as a family of four, each person is only likely to win 25 per cent of the time. That means that they are experiencing failure 75 per cent of the time. Failure might seem like a heavy word in this context, as losing a game is not the worst thing that could happen, but dealing with multiple mini losses really helps to normalise not coming out on top. There will always be someone who is better than you at, well, everything. Unless you're an Olympic gold medallist or a Nobel Prize winner, you don't have to look too far to be beaten in a given domain. When you play games, you learn to compare your performance against your own past performance, rather than always measuring yourself against other people.

It is rare to focus exclusively on a game's end result. Post-game chat often centres around the decisions made during play. These decisions are mulled over and pulled apart. Individuals reflect on the choices they made and the impact those choices had on their success. They make notes to themselves about tactics to tweak, how to learn from others and how to tackle future plays differently. It is common for families to decide to play again immediately to put these thoughts into practice quickly. Game playing normalises persistence and resilience, attributes which are also drawn upon away from the game table. Creative projects go through multiple iterations, improvement in a sport requires repetitive practice and performing to your full ability at school requires application and commitment.

In co-operative and semi-co-operative games, the only way to succeed is to work effectively as a team. Depending on the family dynamics, it can take a concerted effort from the parents to get siblings to work together without competition, but when the metagame is in full swing and the skills of teamwork have been honed and well-practised, this starts to be reflected in other areas. This happens incrementally and may go unnoticed, but one day one of your children will come home from school truly astonished by the others' lack of teamwork. Peers' petty behaviour, angling for control and disruption will be so noteworthy to your child that it will suddenly become clear how much their own skills have developed. Teachers or other parents may start to comment on the maturity or sensibleness of your children. What has, by increments, become normal in your home, may appear so unachievable to others that they'll accuse you of parenting wizardry. Don't get me wrong, your children will still argue with each other and they'll still exhibit behaviours you'd rather not see, but they will learn how to behave in teams, and they'll use that understanding in appropriate situations.

The tactics that we use at the game table spill into other areas of family life. The way we negotiate which games to play helps us to make other joint decisions as a family. The expectation that everyone will help pack games away has an impact on clearing up after meals. Formalised turn-taking teaches patience and encourages a sense of fair play that is apparent as one child waits for another to finish before launching into their own thoughts during a discussion.

Playing good games teaches us that there are multiple ways to win. Some games have several different winning conditions. For example, *7 Wonders Duel* (an excellent two-player game) features three ways in which players can win: military victory, science victory and civil victory. Other games are asymmetric, with players having different abilities or different roles that have different winning conditions – for example, the game *Root* features four different woodland factions, each with different objectives and abilities. Even when a game has a single victory condition – often getting the most victory points – it is clear that there are multiple ways to achieve this goal. You learn to look at the decisions that other players take and not feel compelled to copy them. You understand that you may be just as successful with your own strategy. This understanding of multiple routes to the same outcome is completely transferrable and helps young people to stick to their own ideas, even if others are vocal about their way being best. Confidence in personal decision-making is developed as strategic thinking improves.

The metagame also teaches people how to *play* as competitors. Yes, you are trying to win, but you are also playing a game. It is supposed to be fun. It doesn't matter if you aren't the best. You can remain friendly and supportive while in competition. We've all come across super-competitive adults. These people seem to care about winning so much that they'll tackle anyone who gets in their way, resort to underhand tactics and grandstand their successes to anyone who will listen. These are adults who were almost certainly brought up with the mantra that winning matters. They may have been given praise and attention only when they won a race, came top in tests or landed the best part in a play. Sadly, these adults are pretty difficult to get on with, don't usually work well in teams and take failure badly. Through the metagame we learn that it is so much better to play to win, but not to need to win.

VICTORY POINTS

- Pay attention to the build-up and fallout of each game played. The metagame lasts a lot longer than the game itself and is much more important.

- Allow players who have had enough to leave the table. Employ creative modifications to let others finish.

- Model the behaviour you want to see. Be cheerful in defeat and humble in victory.

- Give recognition and genuinely warm praise to members of your family when they triumph.

- Be prepared to deal with inappropriate behaviour calmly and consistently. Don't allow one person's behaviour to disrupt the whole game.

- Relentlessly teach your family that they should play to win, but not *need* to win.

CHAPTER 5

HOUSE RULES

Make up your own rules to improve game playing.

You only have to play *Monopoly* with another family to understand the importance of house rules. Does landing on free parking allow you to scoop up all the fines from the middle of the board? Do you allow players to negotiate rent payments? What happens when someone doesn't want to purchase a property they land on? Do you have to travel once around the board before you can purchase properties, or can you buy them up straight away? For most people, what it says in the actual *Monopoly* rule book is totally irrelevant: the house rules are law. So much so that Hasbro released a *Monopoly House Rules* version in 2014, with five common house rules, as voted for by players, added.

With board games that have been played in the family for years, house rules may have been passed down through generations. There are so many different versions of Rummy that it is possible that every family plays a slightly different version. When we play, we are allowed to 'buy' the top card from the discard pile when it isn't our turn to pick up. Players who are due to have a turn before the player who wishes to buy must grant permission. If it is their turn next, a player can block the buy, but then they have to take the card themselves. Or anyone else can buy it. To buy a card, you take the card you want and then take a second, face-down card from the top of the draw pile. You get the advantage of the card you want, but you also now have a disadvantage – you have nine cards in your hand instead of seven. There is no limit to the number of cards you can buy, but you have to put them all down to finish. In our family, this variation goes with the added house rule that if you know you are about to complete your hand, and a player asks to buy, you give them the heads-up by saying 'don't buy'. This must, however, be delivered in a supercilious and affected manner – as perfected by Grandma many decades ago.

It is possible for guests to get incredibly irate if house rules are revealed midway through a game, thereby putting them at a perceived disadvantage, but if you take time to brief any visitors before game play begins, house rules are brilliant.

WHY YOU MIGHT NEED HOUSE RULES

Most board games are designed for a wide audience, so you might need to modify things just a bit to suit your family. A glance at the outside of the box will give you some universal information: the number of players, the advised age range and the length of the game. But this information may not be particularly useful. Yes, it will tell you whether you *can* play with two players, but it won't tell you whether the two-player version is inferior to playing it with more people and involves a very unconvincing dummy-hand mechanism that has been crowbarred in, just so they can advertise it as suitable for two players or more (*7 Wonders*, I'm looking at you!). It will tell you that the game is suitable for ages 12 and over, but once you've played it, you realise that your 9-year-old could have coped with this at least three years ago because it builds on the concepts of area control and resource management that he is already very familiar with. The game length usually refers to an average-size group that knows the game well and doesn't spend too much time thinking about their moves. So it is possible that even if you've read the box and think the game will be suitable, it might not work as well as you'd hoped when it hits your table. House rules could be your solution.

Let's take a really simple rule: who goes first. According to the rules, this is often the youngest player. Unless you're constantly having children, this gives someone in the family the advantage, always, forever. Even when they come back home from university for Christmas, they're still the youngest; only the birth of the next generation can change this. Some games have the oldest player starting first (though these are often those in which starting is a disadvantage). *Azul* gives the first player token to the person who last visited Portugal. Having gone to Faro for a girls' weekend in 2016, I retained this privilege until earlier this year when we spent a week in Lisbon as a family. My younger son, Bertie, sneakily choreographed our departure so he was the last to step onto the plane, making him officially the last of the family to visit Portugal and hence gaining perpetual first-turn advantage. We have a house rule to universally ignore all starting player rules and select randomly every time, though I think ingenuity has earned Bertie the right to be to be first player in *Azul*.

USING HOUSE RULES TO ADAPT GAME LENGTH

At the risk of upsetting fans who think that working within the confines of prescriptive game length is a key part of developing an effective strategy, I believe that when playing with your family, it is better to adapt a game so that everyone has the most satisfying experience possible. Sometimes the rule-book conditions might work perfectly for you, but other times the game may be frustratingly long or frustratingly short. Here are some ideas to counter this:

- **Increase or reduce the number of rounds.** Games like *Small World* and *Photosynthesis* are designed to finish after a certain number of rounds have been completed. Why not add in an extra rotation of the sun to allow more trees to be harvested in *Photosynthesis*? Or remove a couple of spaces on the turn marker in *Small World*, so you don't have to put your Bivouacking Ratmen into decline?

- **Restrict or increase resources to modify game length.** When the endgame is triggered through resources running out, add or remove them to change the length of play. *Dominion* ends when the Province cards have all been purchased. Instead of playing *Dominion* with ten Province cards, play with six, or fourteen (to make more Provinces, put a small sticker on a couple of the abundant Estate cards to change the value). *Ticket to Ride* ends when one player has run out of trains. If you remove trains from the game there will be less competition for key routes, players will be able to complete fewer tickets and endgame will be reached sooner. *Carcassonne* ends when the tile stack is depleted. Reduce the number of tiles in play to shorten the game, or add more from expansion packs for a longer game.

- **Change the victory conditions.** If endgame is reached by a player achieving a certain number of victory points, increase or decrease the victory points required for a win to alter the game length. Aim to reach 25 victory points in *Splendor*, not 15, for example. You might wish to shorten the length of your *Catan* games, particularly when playing with more people, and particularly those prone to analysis paralysis. Do so by requiring players to achieve only eight points instead of the prescribed ten.

- **Change the endgame conditions.** Some games finish when one player has managed to construct a certain number of things – for example, buildings in *Havana*, districts in *Citadels*, or scorecards in *Century Spice Road*. Being the player to trigger endgame doesn't automatically make you the winner. Increase or decrease the number of items needed to alter the game length.

Sometimes house rules can be imposed mid-game to increase or reduce the playing time. For example, a long game of *Trivial Pursuit* could be sped up if only one player has any cheese after an hour of playing. (In our house, we call the wedges 'cheeses' but, of course, you might have a different name in your family lexicon.)

Winning the game.

- Either: Players entering the centre with all their cheeses have to answer a question in a category chosen collectively by the other players.
- Or: Players entering the centre with all their cheeses have to answer a question correctly in a self-selected category.
- Or: Players entering the centre with all their cheeses win. No question is asked.

Dice throws.

- Either: Players must land the dice exactly on the centre of the board to take the question at the end of the game.
- Or: Players only have to pass the dice over the centre to take their question at the end of the game.

Re-roll spaces.

- Either: The re-roll spaces are just for re-rolling and nothing else.
- Or: The re-roll spaces allow you to choose whether to re-roll or to immediately move to the closest cheese-winning space.

Acquiring cheeses.

- Either: Players must answer two questions of that colour correctly to get the cheese.
- Or: Players are only able to get a cheese of the colour of the cheese-winning space they are on.
- Or: Players can choose what colour cheese they get when they correctly answer a cheese-winning question.

Regular questions.

- Either: Answering regular questions correctly enables you to re-roll the dice and continue your turn.

🎲 Or: When players answer three questions correctly in a row, they are awarded a cheese of the colour of the final question.

It isn't possible to alter the length of all games, however – at least not without compromising game play or making so many adaptations that it becomes a different game. Deduction games that rely on discovering the answer are hard to adjust for time. Playing **Cluedo** with only two murder cards just doesn't work (I've tested it). You might well play **Scotland Yard** twice in a row with the first game lasting ten minutes and the second lasting forty, but it would be hard to engineer these conditions as the game is centred around how long Mr X can evade capture. Yes, you can restrict or increase the transport tickets that are available to Mr X and to the police, but this usually imbalances the game in favour of one side or the other. That doesn't, however, mean that these games can't benefit from other house rules.

USING HOUSE RULES TO LEVEL THE PLAYING FIELD

House rules can help to level the playing field in games that would otherwise give older players an advantage. Deduction games often require a methodical approach, clear note-taking and carefully considered tactics. My youngest loves to play **Cluedo**, but unless I throw the game – which I refuse to do on principle – I will always win. If the situation is similar in your household, introduce a house rule about differentiated starting conditions. In the initial set-up, the younger or less-experienced players are given more cards. When players have developed their tactics, their handicap is reduced. Alternatively, change the victory conditions for younger players, requiring them to discover only two out of three murder cards correctly to win, for example. You could also give them a very limited number of homemade 'interrogation cards', which they could choose to play at any time during the game. By using these cards on another player, they can force that player to reveal what they know about a certain item. Interrogation cards can also be used in **221b Baker Street**, a deduction game in which players move around the streets of London, seeking to discover clues to solve a crime. Instead of just consulting the case book, younger players could play an interrogation card to consult with another player and force them to reveal the knowledge that they have gained.

Instead of making conditions easier for younger players, try restricting the play of older players. Take *Guess Who*, a very simple deduction game in which the two players have to work out which character the other has selected. The game is aimed at children, and most adults get bored pretty quickly when playing by the standard rules. Here are some ideas to level the playing field and retain the interest of an adult when playing with a child:

- **Make some 'condition cards'.** These are only for the adults. Conditions might include, 'Ask a question using only two words', 'Ask a question about the last letter in their name' or 'Ask a question about their left ear.' The adult must only ask conditions-based questions.

- **The child can lie once.** Play as normal, but once – and only once – during the game, the child is allowed to give the wrong answer. The adult will need to keep all characters face up and will need to make notes to keep track of possibilities. This is pretty challenging!

- **The adult plays without a board.** This version relies on the fact that the adult has probably played the game tens (if not hundreds) of times before and knows the characters as well as they know their own family. The game must be played by making notes about which characters are in and out without looking at the character cards. A more advanced version of this would require the adult to play with no board, no paper and no pen, just using their memory.

- **Place conditions on the outcome of questions.** The adult must knock out (or keep in) an exact number of people on each question. Before they ask a question, the adult rolls a die to see how many characters they are required to knock out (or keep in) that turn. For instance, if the adult rolls a four, they have to ask a question which only four characters could answer yes to – for example, 'Does the name have an E at the end?' could be asked if there are only four characters standing who meet this condition. Adults have to carefully plan their questions or they won't meet the conditions, thereby losing the game.

- **The child takes two character cards.** The adult has to deduce which two cards the child has hidden, but still only using one board. Every question must give yes-or-no answers – for example, 'Are both of your characters smiling?' or 'Do either of your characters have a beard?'

Games of speed and/or dexterity might also disadvantage the youngest or oldest players in your group as response times and motor skills will be key to success. You can add in some fun rules that level the playing field with these too. *Jungle Speed* is a game in which players race to pick up a totem when certain cards are played. Try adapting this by making the most able-bodied touch their head first before grabbing the totem. In *Meeple Circus*, which involves using wooden miniatures to create a circus show, restrictions are placed on players during the final round. Use some of the restrictions that usually only come into play at the end of the game to disadvantage the most dextrous earlier on. For example, make each adult play one round using only one hand, or with one eye covered. These house rules can also be used in *Junk Art*, another dexterity-focused tower-building game.

USING HOUSE RULES TO KEEP EVERYONE IN THE GAME

It is easy to get fixated on the importance of winning a game. It certainly is very satisfying to win – you may get a rush of endorphins, a feeling of smug satisfaction and possibly just a touch of schadenfreude. But what about the flip side? What happens when you lose? Do you feel anger, betrayal or envy? And how do you feel about the winner? An ungraceful win may even provoke feelings of hatred. While most adults can manage these emotions, it is harder for young people to rise above it, especially when the writing is on the wall while the game is still in play. Knowing you are losing and stand very little chance of making a comeback is all the worse when your sister knows that she is winning and loudly eulogising about her astounding strategic decision-making and tactical wizardry.

When embarking on a game, it is easy to get caught up in the initial enthusiasm and promise of what is possible. Even when reminded about what happened last time a particular box was brought to the table, it is normal for children to convince you that there will be no such ugly scenes today. After all, at the start of the game, everyone is level, anyone can win. But some games are more painful than others. It is possible to lose at *Monopoly* for a solid two hours, inching closer and closer towards despair with every roll of the dice.

Game night is so much more harmonious when the scores stay level for longer, when there are no runaway leaders snowballing their way to victory. Many modern games designers avoid snowballing by using 'rubber banding' techniques. Rubber banding means that as the disparity in standings gets larger, the harder it is to increase it, and the easier it is for the losing players to snap back into contention. Catch-up mechanisms can eliminate the feeling of inevitability and make everyone believe they are still in the game. Rubber banding also reduces the cockiness of the current leader, as they know that their position is rocky, and their cruise to victory may easily be derailed.

Some games that have excellent rubber banding features include **Suburbia**, in which you are building a city, but the bigger it gets the harder it becomes to maintain it and its reputation. In **Power Grid**, each player represents a company that owns power plants and tries to supply electricity to cities. It has a great mechanism for punishing players who rush by forcing them into weaker positions in the bidding and purchasing turn-taking order. **Munchkin** has a powerful and often unavoidable 'take that' element, allowing players to gang up to bring down a leader.

I love games that keep the scores secret, or at least partially hidden. Having no clue who is winning really helps players to stay engaged. Often these games are based around individual player boards or tableaux. While you might be able to see other players' tableaux being constructed and look at the options they are taking, you will probably be much more interested in your own board. In **Dice City** and in **7 Wonders**, players compete for the same resources to develop their cities, but the options are plentiful. The same is true of **Shakespeare**, a game in which players hire actors, build sets and create costumes to put on a show. The actors, technicians, props and costumes all come from a central supply, which players select from to develop their own production. These games are described as 'point salads' because points can be picked up in a multitude of ways and there are many different strategic options and ways to win. In point salad games, scoring usually takes place at the end. It is normal to be really surprised about who wins or loses. It is not unusual in our house for my son, Bertie, to leave the table and let the rest of us calculate the scores. It may be over an hour before he wanders back in to ask how he did. This is only possible when the scoring is detached from the game play and doesn't impact on players' enjoyment of the game.

Modifying the official scoring to reduce arguments and increase harmony at the table can work for many games. Let's take another look at the card game Rummy, for example. Rummy is a traditional set-collection game played with one or two standard decks of cards. There are lots of different versions of Rummy and the name is a sort of catch-all for all the different variations. If you don't know it, it is a great card game, simple to learn and easy to play with a range of abilities. You'll find the rules of the version that I play with my family on The Dark Imp blog.[1]

---

1   Ellie Dix, How to play Rummy, *The Dark Imp* [blog] (27 February 2019). Available at: http://www. thedarkimp.com/games-puzzles/how-to-play-rummy/.

In Rummy, players compete to get the lowest score. Unfortunately, if luck isn't on your side, it is possible to get a very high score: you could easily score 50 points on a single round. If the leader is on 0 and the other players are in single figures, this can be pretty demoralising. If you hit 100 points, which might happen after two or three bad rounds, then you are out of the game and play continues without you. When you are familiar with the game, the following scoring adjustments may be useful to keep the playing field more level for longer. You can modify other games using similar methods.

- **Use weighted scoring.** Instead of totalling up the card values to give the score, award the first player 0 points, the second 1 point, the third 2 points and so on. Set a much lower endgame target – perhaps 10 or 15 points, depending on the player count. This keeps the field much closer together.

  Most games with multiple rounds can be scored in the same way. If you're playing Backgammon, for example, just award 1 point for a win, rather than adding up the score.

- **Introduce the 'buy in'.** Allow players who have gone bust by getting more than 100 points to 'buy in' at the next highest score. So, if the others are at 56, 43 and 12 points respectively, the busted player 'buys in' at 56 points. A mark is placed on the scoreboard to signal a buy-in. Play continues as normal. Every player is allowed to buy in once, but as the game progresses the scores that players buy in at get higher and higher, reducing the advantage each time. It is certainly possible for the player who has bought in first to go on and win the game.

  The 'buy in' works well for any game that's scored within short rounds.

- **Set a maximum score.** Cards are totalled as before, but high scores are capped, say, at 20 points. This reduces the damage that a very unlucky round can cause.

  You can set 'maximum damage' for lots of different games. With area control and fighting games, this may fundamentally change players' strategy, however, so maximum damage house rules should be agreed at the start of the game.

- **Use a joker.** Every player is issued with a joker or wild card. This could be an actual joker from the pack, or some other token. Once per game each player may choose one round in which to play their joker. When a joker is played, that round doesn't get added to the player's score. Players can only do this once per game, so must decide when to use it wisely.

Jokers can be used to modify scores in all sorts of different ways in different games: to double points for a chosen move or to reduce losses.

Allow a 'mulligan'. Once per game, immediately after the cards have been dealt, a player can choose to 'mulligan' their hand. This means that they forfeit the hand they have been dealt and take the next seven cards from the top of the deck. Each player can only do this once per game. Discarded hands should be shuffled back into the deck before play starts. You can choose to penalise players for choosing to mulligan by requiring them to draw a hand of eight cards instead, making it a little harder for them to play their whole hand out.

Any game with cards, tiles, dice, tokens, etc. that are all taken at random and visible to the player can use a mulligan. Switch out all your dominoes before the round starts or re-roll your *Yahtzee* dice once per game.

Deal a Rummy dummy. Each round, deal one more hand than the number of players. The extra hand becomes the dummy. At the start of the round, players are permitted to pay to use the dummy hand. Payment is made by adjusting their score. If a player selects the dummy hand, they immediately add five points to their score, and their original hand is shuffled back into the deck prior to play.

The dummy hand can be used in any game in which players start with a random allocation of cards or resources from a larger pool.

Introduce seasons. Instead of playing on when one player has gone bust, end the game at that point. Then score the game. As with weighted scoring, the winner of the game gets 0 points, second place gets 1 and so on. When you've scored the game, start a new one. When that game ends, you can add the score to the season's standings. Seasons can play over a week, a month or any time frame you want. You can decide to close a season if one player becomes a runaway leader or is trailing a long way behind.

Use seasonal scoring for games that the family play repeatedly.

Secret scoreboard. Usually players openly share their score at the end of each round, but an alternative is to keep the scoreboard secret. One player keeps track of the scores (this is usually an adult, although it can be a child if they are particularly good at playing the metagame). Players reveal their score only to the scorekeeper. The scorekeeper may choose to reveal the scores at intervals throughout the game, but they may choose not to – only revealing the winner at the end. Busted players can continue to play as normal, without anyone (possibly even themselves) knowing that they are bust.

- **Beat yourself.** Players compete against their own score from the last time they played instead of competing with each other. Yes, scores are recorded, but the important thing is considering your own performance compared to this time last game. How close to your all-time high score can you all get? We know that people will play on apps and video games for hours just trying to beat their own high score – losing doesn't matter in this context. It is much easier to lose to yourself, clearly due to your previous brilliance, than it is to someone else.

- **No scores.** Just don't keep track of the scores. You play exactly as you normally would, you get the pleasure of winning a round or the frustration of a loss, but there are no overall standings. Each round is played just for fun.

Play about and see what works for you, then introduce successful modifications to your house rules. Of course, these ideas are not limited to Rummy and can be applied to many different games.

USING HOUSE RULES TO IMPROVE GAME PLAY

You know you've got a good game if the minute you finish it, you want to play it again. On the flip side, if packing the game away is a blessed relief, you've got a game that needs to be adapted (or possibly discarded). For me, games that are reliant on pure luck require adaptation as they don't hold my attention for long. In pure luck games, there are very few decisions to make and even if you manage to win, it isn't through good game play, but down to the roll of the dice. Any game in which you can leave the table, go to the loo or make a cup of tea while other people 'play for you' falls into this category. Just making a few modifications can significantly boost interest levels, keeping you away from the kettle and adding a much-needed twist to a pedestrian game.

We own *Game of Life: Adventures Edition*. Normally a game like this would not last that long in our house, but it has survived the chop because, firstly, everyone loves the tokens, which are little model cars. There is something truly lovely about having children and pets and putting them in the back of the miniature cars. In this version, you can also turn your car into a boat or a plane, which is even better. Secondly, it has a cool multipurpose spinner in the middle of the board. You spin to see how many spaces to move, you spin to win money and you spin to discover the outcome of stories. Not only that, but you can also push down on the spinner and move the tracks on the board, changing the available squares and the prices of the houses. Thirdly, it is a classic. Lots of people love it and it might get some reluctant players to the table. But even with these positives, my interest is lost pretty quickly, and the game is therefore an ideal candidate for house rules.

For me, one of the most exciting bits of the game is when you choose a career. This only happens once towards the start of the game, then you're stuck with it. Maybe this was the case when the game was created, but a 'job for life' is now a thing of the past, so why not create a house rule that allows career changes? To change career, you must forfeit your payday and instead return to the career track. You can also go back to college, should you wish, to improve your chances of a better career. Other house rules might include:

- When players purchase a house, they are able to claim one of the ten 'spin to win' places as an extra bonus, increasing their chances of winning a sweepstake until the house is sold again.

- Adding instructions to blank squares - for example, 'Your kid gets fed up with you and runs off to another family' or 'You are envious of your neighbour's car. Follow them around the board and copy all their actions for the next ten minutes.'

- Add a 'space space', which allows you to transform your car into a rocket and orbit the board in the opposite direction at double speed. You go the wrong way around the board and count two spaces for each one. You remain 'in space' until another ten years have passed in the game play.

- Deal out three story cards to each player at the start of the game. When players land on a blank space, indicating that a story card is played, they select from one of the three in their hand. When they've played it, they pick up a new card. They need to keep three in their hand until the cards run out.

One game of chance that is gathering dust in houses everywhere is *Snakes and Ladders*. Here are some ideas for house rules which can be integrated or, in some cases, used independently to improve the action in this nostalgic but otherwise tedious game:

- **Introduce objectives.** Find or make a stack of cards featuring the numbers 1–100. Shuffle the deck and turn the top card over. This number becomes the *goal*. The first player to reach this square claims the card, then another is revealed. The winner is not the person who arrives at 100 first, but the person who collects the most cards. The game ends either when the objective cards have all been claimed or when all the players reach the end of the board.

- **Allocate personal goals.** Deal out three 1-100 cards to each player. These are personal goals which are kept hidden and then revealed to opponents when the player hits that space. A player achieving an objective should pick up a new number card. Everyone keeps three cards in their hand at all times, until the pack is empty or someone has reached the end of the board.

- **Add a track extension.** This moveable extension can be shifted from the end of one line to another. It adds a new loop that players must travel on if they reach that section of the board. The loop can be moved to a different location when a player meets a certain condition - for example, sliding down a snake. The disadvantage they receive also gives them the advantage of shifting the loop to potentially disadvantage their opponents.

- **Add counters on certain squares.** When a player lands on a square with a counter, they can collect it. Counters can be played at any point to block ladders or snakes for a limited time frame - for example, until everyone has taken two turns.

- **Add more dice.** Use a blank die (available very cheaply online) or put stickers over one you already have. Mark the faces with: 'add 1', 'subtract 1', 'move a player one space', 'swap a card', 'change the goal' and 'move the loop'. The player can choose to perform the action or not.

- **Give players choices.** Each throw of the dice can be used as a forward or backward move. For example, if you throw a five, you can choose to go forwards or backwards by five spaces.

- **Play in teams.** Each time the team rolls their dice, they decide which of their players' pieces to move. They don't win until all players are safely over the finish line.

- **Players plan their route.** They write down a combination of four snakes and/or ladders at the start of the game and get extra points if they are able to travel on these in the order that they predicted.

Alternatively, create an entirely new game using the *Snakes and Ladders* board. Experiment by covering up all the numbers and having players start from opposite corners. What is the aim of the game? How do the players move? What do they need to accomplish?

USING HOUSE RULES TO MAKE GAME PLAYING MORE HARMONIOUS

Some games cause arguments no matter what. Some games are actually designed to do that, so these may be best avoided! But you might find that other games benefit from a just a little tweak to improve the likelihood of pleasant play in your household.

- **Removing 'take that'.** I'm not suggesting that games like *Cash 'n Guns* or *Munchkin* which revolve around take-that mechanisms should be modified; that would ruin those games. But there are other games which involve small elements of take that which can be adjusted, without completely changing the game. For example, one *Board Game Geek* user says that her family plays two different versions of *Ticket to Ride* with three people: 3-Normal and 3-Friendly.[2] 3-Normal follows the prescribed rules where no double routes are allowed in the three-player game. 3-Friendly ignores the double-route restriction. It shifts the game a bit, as players are competing for tickets rather than tracks. There are fewer tears – at least until the tickets are revealed.

- **Give everyone a chance to get started.** The early acquisition of resources is really crucial in some games. In *Catan*, players each choose starting positions on a map, at which they will build their two settlements. Resources are acquired according to the type of land surrounding the settlements. Timber comes from woodland, for example. There is strong competition for the best starting positions, and some players may find themselves short of crucial resources early on in the game. Each field has a number corresponding to numbers on the dice. Only when the relevant number is thrown does the field produce resources for the surrounding settlements. Having a few bad turns at the start of *Catan* – if the dice throws don't go your way – can seal your fate at the bottom of the pack, while others gain resources and are able to claim more land and hem you in. This can be very demoralising. In this example, try giving players extra resources at the start of the game so everyone can start the game running.

---

2   See https://boardgamegeek.com/geeklist/150548/whats-best-house-rule-youve-ever-played.

Reducing tension. There is a wonderful two-player card came called Brigadier that my mum absolutely refused to play with my dad for one simple reason. The game includes knocking. The knock – a loud rap on the table – is administered by your opponent if you make a mistake during your turn that they happen to notice. The threat of the knock adds a layer of tension so thick that Mum refused to play. Now, I love the knock, but if Dad had swapped it for a gentle word, he might have got Mum to the game table.

Adding choice. Try adding a drafting phase for any game in which cards – or other components – are dealt out resulting in each player having different hands. To draft cards, deal out the right number to each player, then each player selects a card they want to keep and passes the rest to the player on their left. Players then choose a card from the selection that are passed to them from the right. This keeps happening until each player has a full hand. This won't work for games that rely on the cards being kept secret from the other players.

USING HOUSE RULES TO CHANGE THE PLAYER COUNT

You may have a game that you love, but that you hardly ever get to play because you don't have the right number of people. With a bit of experimentation, you might find that you can create some house rules that effectively modify the game for your number. Try **Scotland Yard** with two players. One is Mr X and the other plays all four detectives. Yes, it's asymmetric, but it works really well and, as there is no negotiation between detectives, it is remarkably quick.

Pictionary can be played with two people if it is converted into a co-operative game. The two players play on the same team, both trying to draw well and guess correctly. They play against the clock, trying to finish in a certain time frame.

Changing the player count in some games takes us more into the realm of game variations than house rules. These can't be described as modifications, but rather are total restructures. For example, Battleships can be played with three people, but you'll need to just use pen and paper and totally ignore the original boards. Print out three 100-squares for each player (you can find these online, or you could draw your own). Mark the squares with the row and column labels 1–10 and A–J. You each draw your ships in one of the grids and use the other two grids for the other players. Take turns to ask questions of the other two players, alternating your questions so that no one is ganged up on. Everyone hears all the responses, so each player is active every turn. Once you've mastered this with three, scale up as desired.

Also try:

- **Connect 3.** Divide your *Connect 4* counters into three piles. Apply stickers of a different colour onto both sides of the counters in one pile to identify them. Each player has a pile of their own colour. Players place a counter in turn and are trying to connect a line of three.

- *Rush Hour* **with two.** This one-player game can be played with two, each player moving one car in turn. You'll need to add special counters that allow players, for a limited number of goes each turn, to play a double move. You could also experiment with one player 'freezing' a vehicle for another player.

- **Four-player Backgammon.** Each player has a home section (half a side of the board). Two players are travelling clockwise, two anticlockwise. Each player has fewer counters than normal. Play as four individuals all jumping on each other, or as two teams, who can protect each other.

House rules can also be used to:

- Patch up broken or forgotten games. For example, I learned a version of Nomination Whist that has three special rounds in the middle of the game – no trumps, misère and … a third round that I can't remember. After a quick think, my husband made up a new round, 'forced bid'. For the forced bid, each player draws a piece of paper at random – from a hat or similar – that tells them how many tricks they are forced to bid that turn. They need to try to achieve that number of tricks.

- Add 'party' elements to strategy games to keep a silly strand running through game play. For example, require all players who are attacking another player to start by saying, 'I'm terribly sorry, my dear chap, but you're rather in my way.' Any attack without this verbal preface becomes illegal.

House rules help to make the game your own. Just as you'd adapt a recipe to create your own twist on a classic Delia, you can add your own ingredients to board games. Playing games is supposed to be fun! If, in adapting a game, you make it more exciting for your family, then it is a good house rule.

VICTORY POINTS

▨ Add creative house rules to prolong the life of your board games and dramatically increase replayability.

▨ Use house rules to tailor games to the needs, interests and personalities in your family.

▨ Introduce asymmetric play to level the playing field for different ages and abilities.

▨ Experiment with extending, adjusting or reworking old classics before you decide to get rid of them.

▨ Take time to explain any house rules to visitors before you play.

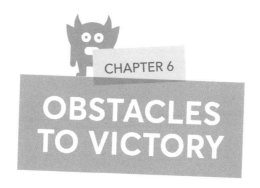

CHAPTER 6

OBSTACLES TO VICTORY

… and how to overcome them.

OBSTACLE 1: ARGUMENTS

'The kids argue as soon as we sit down. I can't get the game going for long enough to put what I've learned into practice!'

Step 1: avoid dangerous games

Not all games are created equal. Just because you've had one relaxed laughter-filled game-playing evening doesn't mean it is plain sailing from then on. At some point you may inadvertently launch into a game that brings out the worst in your family. This can feel like a bomb going off and the table may well end up looking like it has. These hazardous games are hiding in every corner, luring in unsuspecting families. Picking your way through the minefield and then defusing the explosive, before donning your hazmat suit to orchestrate a full-scale clean-up, can be a game in itself.

What follows are my top five dangerous games. In my opinion, these should only ever be embarked on when the sun is shining and everyone is in an utterly charitable mood.

1 **Scattergories.** The king of the monster argument. Games almost always end messily and often with every player barricaded in a different room of the house, counting to ten very slowly. *Scattergories* is lethal because it is a seemingly fun and simple party game, but that is all an elaborate front. Game play involves players thinking of a word or phrase that starts with a certain letter and fits into a given category. For example, a

colour beginning with S might be scarlet. But would 'sky-blue pink' be an acceptable answer? What about sea green? Or siren red? Herein lies the problem. If there are disputes about whether an answer is valid or not – which there invariably are – then the majority decision rules. The 'game' revolves around arguing your case and screaming at people who disagree with you. This, combined with the pressure of having to think of ever more brilliant answers within a strict time limit when you are already seething and preoccupied with shooting death stares at your brother, does not a pleasant evening make.

Also watch out for:

- *Taboo* – 'That was a STUPID clue … and don't put that buzzer next to my ear!'
- *Scrabble* – 'Is that actually a word?'

2 **Diplomacy.** As one *Board Game Geek* forum-user put it, 'Dimplomacy [*sic*] doesn't start arguments so much as decade-long feuds.'[1] This is a game of European domination, in which you can only succeed by making alliances with other nations and then subsequently breaking them. Except if you are Italy. If you are Italy, you are playing at such a disadvantage that you really have no chance at succeeding anyway. The game takes three hours, at least, and much of this time is spent waiting for people who have gone off to another room to discuss alliances (or to pretend to discuss alliances) to return. To top it all off, you could be losing from very early on in the game, without much chance of an amazing comeback. Even if you are winning, you'd have to be pretty hard-hearted to enjoy the game when there are so many miserable people surrounding you. Backstabbing and betrayal are the lifeblood of the game and it's easy for the blood to spill into family relationships. We had a copy of *Diplomacy* when I was a child. We only played it once.

Also watch out for:

- *Intrigue* – 'But I gave you a massive bribe to do that.'
- **Risk** – 'You told me those armies were there for defence!'

3 **Werewolf.** This is a deception game that leaves you wondering whether you can trust anyone any more. Players are secretly assigned different roles and they have to discover the werewolf in the pack before it kills them. The better you are at lying, the more likely you are to win. You

---

1 See https://boardgamegeek.com/thread/1398030/which-game-causes-most-arguments/page/3.

need to convince the other players that they should trust you, even if they can't. While this doesn't seem to cause a problem between friends, when couples or families play together the deception is much harder to take. Spouses, shocked at how easily convinced they were, end up wondering what else they've been lied to about. Siblings become paranoid and unable to forgive and forget. Only bring this to the table if you are prepared to never look at your family in the same way again.

Also watch out for:

- *The Resistance* – 'You seriously don't trust me? After all we've been through!'

- *Munchkin* – 'I can't believe you're using the Kneepads of Allure on me – after I used my Boots of Butt Kicking to help you defeat the Level 20 Plutonium Dragon.'

4 **Bridge.** In theory it is great – a simple concept with a complex strategy that keeps you engaged for years and years. There are lots of good points about Bridge, but you'd have to have a robust relationship to withstand a Bridge partnership. Bridge relies on silent communication between partners, who are playing independently but together. It would really help if you had X-ray vision or psychic powers, but for us mere mortals, we need to rely on our best predictions to know what cards our partner is holding. Even if you've been playing with the same partner for years, there are so many ways to make mistakes, they are completely unavoidable. The co-dependence on your partner's play is a hotbed of potential disputes. Several Bridge partnerships have even ended in murder.[2] I rest my case.

Also watch out for:

- *Hanabi* – 'Well, you never told me I had that!'

- *The Mind* – 'Why would you only wait five seconds to play number 63?'

5 **Monopoly.** Everyone has a disastrous *Monopoly* story to tell. The player in the lead may be thoroughly enjoying the game, but at the expense of all others, whose demise can be oh so painfully slow. In 2016, Hasbro even set up a *Monopoly* Helpline at Christmas to help families solve their disputes. A board game with a helpline – enough said.

---

2 Search the internet for the case of Myrtle and John Bennett, for example.

Step 2: find the triggers

My top five dangerous games are explosive because of the mechanisms they employ: deception, debate, co-dependency without communication, runaway leaders, alliances and backstabbing. But sadly, these are not the only things that cause arguments. As you play, try to find the triggers that upset, anger or worry your family. Each person is different, but here are a few things to look out for:

- Players who whine about being attacked or badly treated often cause other players to treat them differently, thereby swinging the game in their favour. Everyone gets so fed up with the moaning that they stop attacking the individual so they don't have to listen to it. The moany player can end up winning, which only perpetuates the problem, because now moaning is seen as a winning strategy. If this happens in your family, tighten your metagame to reframe destructive behaviours.

- Teaching the rules gradually to new players really helps to get games started quickly, but revealing rules as a player is about to break them can cause trouble. Equally, performing a tactically brilliant move before you explain that it is legal will attract huffy mutters. Castling in Chess is a good example of this.

- Players interfering with the 'spirit' of the game will undoubtedly spark a row. These are strategies that are perfectly legal within the rules but that give the player an unfair advantage. You will certainly win **Ticket to Ride** if your strategy is just to claim routes that others want while taking minimum tickets, but it won't make you any friends.

- Games that give some players an advantage because of their depth of knowledge are not really suitable for playing as a family unless they are adapted. Playing **Trivial Pursuit** using the same cards for adults and children is just mean. Unless you employ some really good house rules to level the playing field, or you've raised child geniuses, younger players don't stand a chance and you may have a full-scale mutiny on your hands.

- When a game is completely reliant on luck for success and the roll of the dice just isn't with someone, the situation could become messy. When players feel that they have no control over their fate whatsoever, they'll quickly lose interest and often become disruptive. When playing *Sorry*, players must draw a 1 or 2 card before they can even start. Cue screams of frustration and accelerating disengagement. The game is over before it has even begun.

◻ Nobody likes sitting around waiting for other players to make decisions. If some of your family are prone to analysis paralysis, which increases the amount of downtime for others, this should be carefully managed. Games that enable you to see many turns into the future, like the tile placement game **Cottage Garden**, may make players want to plot their next four or five moves before they make a move this turn. Cue collective rage!

◻ Sharing information about your cards, your game plan or your short-term tactics can be fatal in some games. Even staring at a certain part of the board may give your opponents information that they can use against you. An innocent, 'Remind me where Windermere is again,' in *The Great Game of Britain* may see another player placing a train signal on this branch of the network, preventing anyone else from entering the Lake District. Not fair. Much crying.

◻ Super-complicated games that require the rule book to be consulted during every round will surely end in fireworks. A game that the box proclaims takes 60 minutes will be accelerating downhill when you enter the fourth hour. Check the size and quality of the rule book before you buy the game (you can get PDFs of most online). If it has 240 pages, uses seven different fonts or loses you in the first paragraph, avoid it!

Step 3: reduce interaction

Games that use individual boards or solo scorecards, or focus on each player building their own tableau, can significantly reduce the number of arguments in feisty families. The presence of the individual board or score-card focuses each player's attention on their own game and away from others'. You may be able to see what other players are doing, but you are much more likely to be interested in your own game.

There are, of course, a huge number of different games that use the tableaux mechanism. The levels of interaction between players will vary. Players may compete for communal resources or the resources may be unlimited. Players may take turns, or everyone might play at the same time, using the same information to make decisions.

Take the humble roll and write genre: the granddaddy of which is **Yahtzee**. In turns, each player rolls the dice, makes decisions about their own play and enters scores in their chosen field. Players are working on their own sheet and the choices of the other players have no impact on their game, until the scores are tallied at the end. It won't prevent the losers being grumpy, but there is no opportunity for players to gang up on each other, or to affect each other's game play: the take-that element is effectively removed.

The ability to make choices in isolation from others allows players to test new tactics and experiment without the weight of others' eyes upon them. You know that you can't be attacked, so you take risks that you might not if playing defensively. Players are effectively striving to beat their own previous score, rather than worrying about the standings.

Try these brilliant roll and writes, in which everyone plays every turn and there is no interaction between players:

- **Welcome to ...** Players become architects in 1950s' America and compete to construct the American Dream.
- **Railroad Ink.** Construct railways and roads to make the biggest network of connections.
- **Rolling Ranch.** Decide where to build your barns and house your pigs, cows and chickens to get the highest scoring fields.

Some other low-interaction games include:

- **Shakespeare.** Players create individual tableaux but compete for communal resources.
- **7 Wonders.** Involves quick card drafting and minimal direct competition. (Card drafting is a mechanism in which you are dealt a hand of cards, you choose one to keep and then pass the rest of the cards to the player on your left, while receiving cards from the player on your right. Each time you receive cards you choose one card and pass the rest on.) Everyone plays each turn.
- **Agricola.** There's competition during worker placement, but it is a great personal tableau builder.
- **Take It Easy.** Everyone works on individual boards with zero interaction. A true multiplayer solitaire game.

Here's the downside … One of the best things about playing board games is the interaction between players. While low-interaction games might help to reduce arguments, they'll also reduce positive collaboration and general discussion. They can be super fun, of course. Just try to take time to talk about everyone's game afterwards and intersperse them with other types of game.

Step 4: team up

Nervous or downtrodden siblings can get stressed if they feel they are under pressure from their brother or sister, who is just waiting for them to slip up, so they can taunt them when they fail. As an adult this might seem like an extreme view of a situation that looks more like friendly ribbing or healthy competition, but even a simple game of *Snakes and Ladders* could be the straw that breaks the child's back in the wrong situation. It is so important that the whole family really enjoys playing games together: when each person is playing for themselves, a supportive and jovial atmosphere is helpful.

Working as part of a team can ease the uglier side of competition that haunts some game play. Look for fully co-operative games and those designed for teams, or adapt your existing collection to suit. Here's a quick overview of what to look out for:

- **Co-operative games.** All players form one team and work together to beat the game. In **Pandemic**, players must control the spread of infection across the world: treating cities, dealing with outbreaks, setting up research bases and searching for cures. Each player has a vital role, but success can only be achieved as a team. **Mechs vs. Minions** sees all players joining forces as different mechs to battle an army of minions in story-driven campaigns that make each mission completely different to the last. **Space Alert** requires players to work together to complete space missions while protecting and repairing their spaceship. Fully co-operative games can often be played face up on the table, at least while everyone is getting familiar with the game. This will enable less-confident players to get advice from the rest of the team about what moves they should make, which will increase the team's overall chances of winning. However, in co-ops, particularly when playing open hands, watch out for an 'alpha player' emerging – someone who may try to take control of everyone's game play by claiming that they know exactly what to do to win. If this happens, consider how you can sharpen your metagame.

- **One versus many.** One player has a different role, and the rest work together against them. **Catacombs** involves one player cast as the overseer, who controls the monsters of the catacombs. The other players control the four heroes who co-operatively try to defeat these monsters and, eventually, the catacomb lord. Each of the heroes has special abilities that must be used effectively if they are to prevail. Other asymmetric games involve one player having a different role, but nobody is sure who the double agent or enemy is: **Room 25** and **Betrayal at House on the Hill** fall into this category. When playing these games, make sure that you take the time to prepare the family for deception and betrayal.

- **Equal teams.** Players are divided into teams and work together with their teammates to defeat the other team. In **Captain Sonar**, up to 8 players can divide into two teams. Each team operates a submarine, trying to keep their location secret while finding and dealing damage to their enemy. Each member of the team has to perform a different role and works from a different section of the submarine bridge. This real-time game can be totally immersive. A large screen placed down the middle of the table separates the teams and heightens the competition and collaboration. **Space Cadets: Dice Duel** is another real-time team game, in which two spaceships are pitted against each other in dice-throwing combat.

- **Two players playing as one.** Most games in which players compete as individuals can also work with two people playing as one. A notable exception to this would be memory games, in which two brains would put the pair at a significant advantage. Paired players can discuss their moves and make decisions together or take it in turns. This might speed up a slower game, provide assistance when learning the rules and developing tactics or make for a more enjoyable experience for less-confident players. Again, take care to avoid an alpha player making every decision for a pair. Also watch out for any games in which open communication might reveal information to opponents.

Playing on a team helps you to learn from other players, and to develop and experiment with strategies supported by your teammates. Less-experienced or more-nervous players can take the role of First Mate in **Captain Sonar**, which means making fewer pressured decisions, while closely observing the other roles and discussing tactics with the team. **Space Alert** involves a timed element and moments when communication is illegal, but you can still make time to check your thinking with other players before potentially making a move that could spell disaster for the team (even if you need to add a house rule that allows the players to pause the action to do so).

OBSTACLE 2: SMARTPHONES

'I can't get my son to leave his phone somewhere else when we're playing.'

The ultimate aim is for your children to badger *you* into playing board games, enthusiastically taking one to the table and playing for a couple of hours, having left their smartphones abandoned in another room. While this is totally achievable, it is unlikely to happen overnight. Our ingrained smartphone-checking habits are strong and need to be reprogrammed. If you expect your family to morph into the Waltons on day one - suddenly becoming wholesome and uncomplicated - just because you've brought out a board game, you may want to adjust your thinking.

Step 1: start with short games

Introduce the idea of concentrating on the game on the table and minimising distractions. It is useful to establish this expectation straight away. But avoid demanding that phones are never brought to the table: absolute bans are hard to stand down from. It is best to avoid confrontation and instead take an approach of subtle reinforcement, positive modelling and engagement by stealth. Start with short games that require concentration and involvement for limited bursts of time. This will give your family the opportunity to successfully put down their smartphones for manageable periods before you build up to tackling longer games. Play real-time games or those with simultaneous action selection to minimise downtime, thereby reducing the amount of unfilled time.

If you are really struggling to get the family to put their smartphones away for the length of the game, use the game flow to provide windows of permitted smartphone-checking. Doing this during a natural pause - at the end of a round, when pieces are being replenished or cards are being shuffled, or when shifting between one game phase and another - will be less disruptive than checking mid-turn.

Step 2: put smartphones on silent

If the soundtrack to your family time is punctuated by the rapid-fire bells and buzzes of push notifications, ask everyone to put their smartphones on silent. Establishing this expectation is easier than fighting with Pavlov's dog on every beep. Your children don't (just) check their notifications to annoy you. It is a routine response that has a powerful subconscious pull. You hear the noise, you check your smartphone. Habit. Without the digital chimes going off, you have a far greater chance of fully engaging everyone in the game.

As a side note, if your children seem like slaves to their smartphones, you can combat this by preventing apps from sending push notifications. I'm not suggesting that you grab their smartphones and deactivate all apps (that's assuming you can get past the parent-proof password). Instead, encourage your children to deactivate the notifications in the apps of their own accord. They can still check the apps whenever they like, and will see the notifications when they are opened. The difference is *choice*. They'll begin to feel more in control of their smartphone, rather than like the smartphone is controlling them. If they are concentrating on something offline, they can get lost in it for a while, without the persistent buzzes snapping them out of it by demanding attention every few minutes.

Step 3: avoid confrontation

Wherever possible, avoid confrontation over phones at the game table. Rigid imposition of rules and ugly showdowns leave long-lasting imprints. If we want our children to willingly and excitedly come to the game table, negative associations need to be avoided as much as possible. Make sure that you are in the right mood before you suggest playing. If you are irritable, preoccupied or overly tired, you're less likely to be able to manage your reaction to behaviour that tests you. We've all been in positions where we've declared a new world order and promised to 'do a Kirstie Allsopp' by smashing up all the devices or turning the Wi-Fi router off by 7pm.[3] Wild claims and hastily imposed bans only serve to release your frustrations. Try to do that away from the game table - at least in the early days while you're

---

3   See Patrick Greenfield, Kirstie Allsopp defends decision to smash her children's iPads, *The Guardian* (15 September 2018). Available at: https://www.theguardian.com/tv-and-radio/2018/sep/15/kirstie-allsopp-defends-decision-smash-childrens-ipads.

hooking the family in. The more involved in the games the family becomes, the less damaging the occasional display of frustration will be. If you lose it, as you inevitably will do at some point, take the time to apologise when you are calm. A genuine apology has a huge impact and can help to restore balance. You are also modelling gamesmanship for the rest of the family.

As you develop your own game-playing rituals, you may decide to ask for phones to be left away from the table, or to be put in the Game Chest in exchange for a personal meeple. Allow these routines to develop over time. You may even find that your children become the guardians of the tech-free table. My sons berate each other if they become preoccupied with their smartphones when they are supposed to be playing. Time put aside for the family to play together is not just important to you, it becomes a routine that the family will treasure and fight to protect.

Step 4: assign roles

Another approach to smartphones at the table is to use them to support the game. Allocate the responsibility for keeping score to one of your children. They can use the calculator and notepad functions or a free app like ScorePal.[4] ScorePal allows you to keep track of scores during each game, and also logs your plays. You can assign different avatars to each player, search for pretty much any board game ever made and use digital copies of the scorecards for that game. You can check back to see previous scores, so you can aim to beat your last score. The app will also tell you when you've achieved a personal high score or even a game best. If you are documenting your game plays, smartphones can be used to take photos, make video and audio recordings and even live-stream the action from your game table.

There is no single right way of managing phones at the table; each family needs to find a solution that works for them. Your effort should go into reducing distractions, whatever that looks like for you. With fewer distractions, there is more interaction among family members and more engagement in game play. The aim is for each player to be fully present within the game.

---

4   See https://scorepalapp.com/.

OBSTACLE 3: MONEY

'We're on a very strict budget and I just can't afford to buy lots of new games.'

Board games can be expensive. There are thousands of sparkly new games on the market every year, many with hefty price tags. So how do you navigate this cave of wonders without breaking the bank? Time for some board-gaming truths …

Truth 1: board game maths gives better odds than fashion maths

Some women's magazines feature what they call 'fashion maths'. They showcase expensive items of clothing, estimate how many times the piece would be worn and then, ignoring the variables, give you the cost per wear. The cost per wear is usually more than I would actually spend on *purchasing* an item of clothing. As a student I became adept at doing my own fashion maths: my paisley skirt from Cambridge market probably cost about 15p per wear, my trusty Levi's about 10p and my charity-shop sweatshirt – only £1 when new (to me) – would be somewhere under the half-penny mark, lower if you count the use after its recommission as a cleaning rag (my style was more unique geek than chic). I may not have won any fashion awards, but board gaming rewards the thrifty eclectic. There are clear trends in game design, and a successful title can inspire a breakout of games on the same theme or centred around the same mechanism. But, as with fashion, the current industry trends don't have that much of an influence on the average family. Keen hobbyists may race out to buy the latest Uwe Rosenberg, Stefan Feld or Jamey Stegmaier release, but many lifelong family gamers wouldn't even know the names of these game designers.

Board games are timeless. Find a game you like and you, your children and your grandchildren will be playing it for years to come. Most games are truly built to last and cope well with grubby fingers, being dropped on the floor and the occasional spillage. Calculating the cost per play of your shelf staples is much more economically satisfying than calculating cost per wear of items in your wardrobe, particularly when you consider how many people participate in each game. The purpose of my game collection is to play with others, but with the notable exception of a long-sleeved grey bodysuit discovered by my sister and I in C&A in 1991 which we subsequently bought to 'share' (it didn't go well), my wardrobe is for me alone. Divide the cost per play by the number of players and you get real value for money. Choose your games wisely and the cup of tea you sip while you play will probably work out costing you more than the game itself.

Truth 2: you don't have to own a game to play it

While you may be keen to add new games to your collection, there are lots of options other than ownership. Start by contacting your local public library; most offer more than just books. Many have collections of games for you to play at the library or to borrow. Some libraries also hold special board game events, even inviting publishers to demonstrate new games. Your library's collection may be limited to mainstream party games, or it might be a rich stream of quirky new releases. It will very much depend on how much the purchasing librarians know about the hobby. The good news is that there is a big crossover community of board-gaming librarians, so you might be lucky!

While those living in Britain's rural extremities might have too far to travel, if you're within easy reach of a city, board-gaming cafes are another good option. For the record, I'm not referring to ordinary coffee shops that happen to have *Guess Who*, **Rummikub** and a heavily graffitied copy of *Trump: The Game* stacked in the corner. Rather, these oases of game-lined walls will rent you a table for several hours and let you try whatever games take your fancy. Staff will not only offer you a pot of tea and a range of toasted sandwiches (the unofficial food of board-gaming cafes), but will also advise you on what games to try. If you want some guidance, they'll ask what you have played before, what games you've enjoyed (and what you've hated) and whether you want to try several quicker games or delve into a weightier box. Most staff will explain rules and help you to get started quickly so that you're not wasting too much time trying to navigate a rule book. It is always advisable to book your table ahead of time as these specialist cafes are busy places. If there are particular games that you'd like to try, you can ask to reserve them.

I love board-gaming cafes and think that the expertise, the range of options and the atmosphere are well worth paying the table rental for, but if you are on a very tight budget, you might find a local board-gaming group suits you better. In every corner of the country, board-gamers from all walks of life meet weekly, fortnightly or monthly in village halls, community centres and even in convents. (I once spent a wonderful day with the warm and welcoming Beyond Monopoly group at the Bar Convent in York.) You may have wondered what the locked cupboard in your church hall contains, and there's a good chance it's packed with board games: the treasure trove of the local game club. The board-gaming community is incredibly inclusive: everyone is welcome. A small entry fee helps towards the hire of the hall, but these are non-profit organisations. Clubs are run by enthusiasts who just want to find others to play with. You can go on your own, with a friend or with your whole family. You'll get the most out of it when you try games you've never heard of and play with all sorts of different people. If you come as a family, you can play together if you want, but it's always fun to form splinter groups and play with others. Collectively, you'll have more experiences to share and discuss afterwards.

To find your local board-gaming clubs, you could do a Facebook group search, as many will broadcast and communicate on that platform. But there is one sure-fire way to find out what is happening close to you. Register for a free account on *Board Game Geek*, the go-to website for the board-gaming community the world over. As well as researching every board game ever published, losing yourself in users' lists of recommendations and checking out which games are in the current top ten (as voted by users), you can tap into your local network through the extensive forums. Navigate to the 'Game Groups' section of the forum and find your country. You'll then see a list of all the discussion groups. You can also search the list for your town or county. If you can't find anything, then just post a message saying where you are and asking if anyone knows of any local game groups. You'll get responses for sure.

Your quest to discover local board-gaming cafes and groups could be extended to find your closest friendly, local game store (FLGS). Each FLGS will stock a variety of board and card games, from old classics to new releases. But while it is fun to browse the shelves, your FLGS has more to offer. Many run demo sessions, which give you a chance to play new games, some run special evenings and tournaments, but, crucially, the owner and staff will have all sorts of knowledge you can tap into and will almost certainly be very well-connected in the area. You may be able to find out about local events, auctions, groups, etc.[5]

---

5 http://findyourgamestore.co.uk/ is a good resource. You'll also see listings for comic shops, but many of these also stock games.

Of course, if you invite friends and family over to play your games with you, you may well get them hooked too. Try to encourage them not to buy the same games as you. If they get different ones, then you'll have two collections, and the start of your very own joint board game library.

Truth 3: your trash is someone else's treasure (and vice versa)

Board games hold their value brilliantly. Have a good look at the games you have on the shelf and do a proper audit. Games that haven't been played for ages, that always end in arguments or that are really unsatisfying adaptations of TV shows are taking up valuable shelf space. As you go through your collection, work out if you've had any really good experiences while playing these games. If you can't remember, the game can probably go. Any game so dusty that you're struggling to identify it can go too. If you have a game that never gets to the table because you have a similar one that is better, it can go. If you bought the new edition of a game from your childhood in a fit of nostalgia, but now realise that the game is – and always has been – rubbish, it can go. If you are keeping a game you've been given, just in case that person asks about it, it can go. If you bought a game for your children when they were 3 and 5 and they are now 16 and 18, it can go. If you bought a game in a charity shop because it was only £1 but half the components are missing, it can go. Get rid. Embrace your inner Marie Kondo. Only keep the games that you are actually going to play. Your game collection is not a museum of the past; it is a gateway to future experiences with family and friends.

Now your to-go pile needs sorting. Firstly, separate out any games that might be worth some money. You may have some old games that are still in their original boxes – these might be two a penny but they could be pretty rare. The value of your newer games will depend on how mainstream they are and what condition they are in. Games that are in mass circulation are unlikely to be worth much, but games that lots of people want to play will be worth more. Games that are very niche might even attract collectors. If you have an original copy of *Fireball Island* – the 1980s release from MB – for instance, you could be sitting on a few hundred pounds.

If you're not sure how much your games are worth, just do a quick search on internet auction sites and on the *Board Game Geek* 'Geek Market', where tabletop gamers sell used copies of games. Any games that really aren't worth selling can either be donated to charity or stripped of components and recycled. If you don't mind boxing up and posting items, listing those games you want to sell on Geek Market will probably get you the best prices. Or if you want a speedier sale, a better option might be to list them on an online auction. Alternatively, board game conventions usually have 'buy and sell' sections for second-hand games.

Once you've cleared a load of shelf space, you can fill it with new games! But how can you make sure that you don't spend too much? Well, you've already made some money from your old games, so you will have a bit of a budget to play with. Plus, now you know that you'll be able to resell games later on, should you wish to. All the places that you've sold to, you can now buy from. If there is a particular game you're looking for, check online auction sites and *Board Game Geek*. Geek Market will give you a good idea of market value. A Google shopping search will bring up results from multiple sellers. Buy from conventions and tell your FLGS or local game group what you are look-ing for – they will help. There are also some very active Facebook groups for people buying and selling games, which are worth checking out.

Charity shops are worth a look too. Check between copies of *Blockbusters* and dated editions of **Trivial Pursuit** and you may find a hidden gem. Most of the time you won't, but sometimes, just sometimes, you'll strike gold. Searching is a game in itself.

Truth 4: you can get new games for free!

There is a huge and ever-growing sub-section of board gaming: Print and Play (PnP) games. These PnP games, as the name suggests, can be down-loaded and printed at home. You'll need an internet connection, a printer and a load of paper. Some games can be printed in black and white, but many require colour, so do check before you print. To make the most of these games you'll also need:

- A good supply of card – to back the cards, board and components.
- Some glue (ideally adhesive spray) – for mounting the components onto the card. (Of course, you could print straight onto the card if your printer allows it.)
- Good quality scissors or a craft knife, a cutting board and a metal ruler – for cutting out accurately.

▪ Dice, tokens and counters (or something that will suffice) – as most PnP games will expect you to have the basic game components to use with the printed elements.

There are thousands of PnP games available for free online. It can sometimes be challenging to search out the best ones, as PnP-only designers don't make money on their games and therefore have limited (read non-existent) resources for marketing. Sometimes you can find free PnP versions of games that are later published. Some designers will release a free PnP version to get feedback from the game-playing community ahead of a release. For example, at the time of writing you can freely download a full PnP version of *Root*, an asymmetrical four-player game that is getting a huge amount of attention.

Board Game Geek's lists and forums are the best place to discover PnP games. Other users who have tried and tested the games will give their opinion and point you in the direction of the best ones. Do a search for 'best PnP games' or 'top free PnP games' to get the latest hot tips. Blog posts on the site often give you the latest releases with links to access the files. Also look at the results of the (many) PnP design contests. The winning games are a good place to start. As well as *Board Game Geek*, check out Button Shy[6] – who create PnP games that use just 18 cards – and Cheapass Games, a game publisher dedicated to providing board games at a cheap price.[7] They do have some titles for sale, but also a good selection of PnP games.

Try:

▪ **Decktet.** A PnP game system. Download and print the deck of cards and then search for all the different games you can play with them.

▪ **Paiko.** A one-on-one duel to out-build, out-position and outmanoeuvre your opponent with a new style of turn-based strategy.

▪ **Grease Monkey Garage.** A one- to five-player game where players are shift managers of a garage and trying to outperform the other managers to become employee of the month.

---

6   See https://buttonshygames.com/.
7   See https://cheapass.com/.

Truth 5: never underestimate the plain old playing card

My luxury *Desert Island Discs* item would be a pack of playing cards. Well, two packs if it's allowed. The International Playing-Card Society estimates that there are between 1,000 and 10,000 card games in existence.[8] True, I'd need to find other castaways to play most of them with me, but even if I remained alone, there are still hundreds of different one-player card games to choose from. I carry playing cards in my handbag all the time. Cheap, light and robust, they can be whipped out in a spare five minutes to fill a hole in your day. Some of the happiest game evenings we've had as a family have revolved around the humble playing card.

From the simple bluffing game Cheat to the in-depth strategy and psychic communication required in Bridge, there are card games to suit everyone. Experiment with different types of games until you have a collection of family favourites.[9] Here is your starter for ten:

▪ **Simple trick-taking.** Knockout Whist (also known as Trumps). Quick, simple and a great way to develop trick-taking skills. Prevent players from being knocked out as easily by playing additional rounds in which the eliminated player is handicapped but has a chance to get back into the game. First they play a round 'blind' (they can't see their cards and have to select which to play at random); failure to win a trick here will lead to 'dogs' (they are only dealt one card, and they have to choose the best time to play it to hopefully win a trick); and finally 'blind dogs' (they are dealt only one card, which they can't see). If they are eliminated after they've played blind dogs, they are out of the game. More than one player may be blind or dogs at any one time, but the number of cards dealt each round is not decreased until all players are fully back in the game or knocked out completely.

▪ **A twist on Whist.** Nomination Whist. In the first round, players are dealt one card. Before they play the hand, each must declare how many tricks they are going to take (in the first round this will be one or none). The final player must declare a number that would make it impossible for every player to achieve their goal. At least one player must fail in each round. Players are given 1 point for each trick taken and 5 points for achieving the exact number of tricks they declared. The number of cards increases as the rounds progress. Special rounds with no trumps

---

8 See https://i-p-c-s.org/faq/games.php.
9 For ideas, see Parlett's *The Penguin Book of Card Games*.

occur later on. Being successful at predicting the number of tricks you will take will win you the game.

- **Set collection.** Rummy.[10] Collect sets of runs of the same suit or cards of the same number and beat your opponents to be the first player to lay all your cards down on the table. Players with cards still in hand count up the points in their hand and add it to their score. Players try to keep their score low because when they hit 100 they are out.

- **Low-level betting.** Newmarket. Players are given a pile of ten matchsticks (or poker chips), with which they bet on 'horses' and pay into the pot to join each round. The horses are represented by four face cards from another pack. A dummy hand is also dealt out, which players can bid for if they don't like their own cards. The person with the two of clubs lays it on the table, and players follow on with clubs of increasing value. When the group hits a gap (due to a card being in the dummy hand rather than in play) the play is switched to the lowest red card in circulation. Players are hoping that their horses will come out so they can collect their winnings before someone puts their last card down and claims the pot. This is a game of pure luck.

- **Introduction to contracts.** Solo Whist. Players take it in turns to bid their contract. Contracts include solo (winning five tricks on your own), prop and cop (winning eight tricks with another player), abundance (winning nine tricks on your own) and misère ouverte (winning no tricks at all with your cards face up on the table). The highest bid contract is the one that is then played out, with the winner of the bid trying to meet the contract to claim points.

- **Simple strategy.** Black Maria. This is a trick-taking game in which all the cards in the deck are dealt out. However, before the trick-taking begins, each player passes on three cards to the person on their left and accepts three cards from the person on their right. Tricks are played as in Whist, but players are trying to score as few points as possible. As in the game Hearts, every heart scores one point. In addition, the ace of spades scores 7 points, the king of spades scores 10 points and the queen of spades (Black Maria) scores 13.

- **Quick maths.** Cribbage. Two players each take a hand of six cards, from which they choose four to play. After play, each hand is analysed and bonus points are scored for pairs, runs and flushes.[11] The delightful

---

10 Dix, How to play Rummy.
11 The rules are really rather complicated, so for a full explanation, see: https://www.mastersofgames.com/rules/cribbage-rules.htm.

cribbage scoring board and pegs, which track your progress to 121, can be picked up easily and cheaply online or from game shops.

- **Crazy speed.** Slam (aka Spit). This is best as a two-player game, as players compete to get their stockpile cards out onto two spit piles in the centre of the table. A card can only be played if its value is one higher or lower than the card on the top of the pile – for example, a 7 could only be placed on a 6 or 8. Any suit can be played. The only restrictions are that you can only use one hand and that you can only move one card at a time. You are limited only by the speed at which you can move and think. Lots of fun, if you don't mind getting slapped by your opponents a bit.

- **Loads of people.** Racing Demon. There is no upper limit to the number of people who can play Racing Demon. It works best with at least 4 players but is really fun with more. You'll need a pack of cards each though! Each person counts out 13 cards, which are placed face down next to them to form their 'demon'. They each turn the top card up. Four more cards are drawn from the deck and placed in a row, face up. Then the race begins. Players turn over the cards in their deck in threes. Any aces revealed go in the middle of the table. Cards of ascending numbers in the same suit can be placed on the growing communal piles in the centre of the table. Players work simultaneously as quickly as they can: there are no turns. The aim is to be the first person to get rid of their demon. This is brilliant, but can get very messy.

I could go on and on … Search YouTube for new card game demonstrations and learn them in minutes. You could play a new card game every day for the next ten years and still not have to repeat one.

Truth 6: mix it and fake it to make it

As you trawl the charity shops in search of that elusive copy of *Star Wars: The Queen's Gambit*, keep your eyes out for any games with loads of components. I picked up a copy of *Yahtzee Texas Hold 'Em* and *Yahtzee World Series* in one shop for a combined price of £1.50. We played the games a few times but then grew disinterested. So I stripped the games of their components: 40 different-coloured dice in total, 4 shakers, a load of poker chips and a pretty cool electronic buzzer thing. The dice have been added to our central supply so that each player can have their own set when playing and we use the poker chips for card games that involve betting – like Newmarket, which I've just described. Personally, I love to design my own games, so it is really useful to have a few bags of counters, tokens, dice and other components that I can recommission as part of a new creation.

When you have a good stack of tactile game components, it is easy to start making up your own games. If this makes you a little nervous, start by making your own versions of games like **Yahtzee**. Make new categories that include different combinations – like 'odds' in which only odd numbered dice are scored, or 'two pair' in which the values on the two pairs are scored. Add a bonus die into the mix to create categories with six dice. Throw in some counters that you can play three times during the game to give you an extra roll or to change one die to a different value. Before you know it, you've created your own game.

You can also create your own versions of traditional games like Chess and Chinese Checkers. Make your own board and create your own pieces. Pull the family in, if you can, and make it a bit of a project. Mancala can be made easily using egg boxes and marbles, as can Bao, a two-player game from East Africa. Search for traditional games from around the world and fashion your own versions of them using old game boxes and decommissioned components.

Aside from cost, another advantage of making your own games is that you can personalise them. Make your Chess pieces resemble members of the family; name your Backgammon points after places that are significant to you; decorate your *Ludo* board with photos of family members making silly faces. Customise old packs of cards (or buy blank ones online) to create your own sets. You can also get card sleeves quite cheaply which let you disguise blemishes on cards and make them all look the same. The sleeves should outlive the cards and can be reused with multiple packs and iterations of games.

Truth 7: you will never play every game available ... so don't try

There are now almost 4,000 new games being released each year, and that doesn't include expansions of established games.[12] If you were to try to play all of this year's releases, you'd be playing more than ten different games every day. Even professional board gamers who make their living from reviews and have games sent to them for free can only tackle a small percentage of new releases. I think this knowledge is very liberating. You can't play everything, so play what you want to play regardless of how 'hot' it currently is. It is possible to bag some bargains by grabbing slightly older titles from board game shops that need to make space for new releases.

So, with so many games available, how do you decide what to spend your money on?

- Select games that really appeal to your family. Is skiing your thing? Choose a skiing game. Love Harry Potter? No problem. Do you have a passion for the constructed language of Italian fabric merchants in the late Middle Ages? Yes, you've guessed it, there's a game for that (*De Vulgari Eloquentia*, in case you're interested).

- Put the names of games you'd like to own in a hat or envelope. Encourage the rest of the family to contribute their ideas too. Weed out rogue suggestions of purchasing *PU: The Guessing Game of Smells* or *Mr. Bacon's Big Adventure*. When you have a bit of spare money, pick a game at random from your selection.

- Conduct a debate. Each member of the family chooses a game they'd like to buy and prepares a brief (two-three-minute) pitch to sell their idea. At the end of the debate, each person votes for a game other than their own and the winning game is purchased. Beware of being outnumbered by children who have agreed to rig the outcome!

- Read reviews, listen to podcasts, watch videos and look at top ten lists. See what captures your attention and that of your family.

---

12 *Board Game Geek* lists around 4,000 games published in 2018 excluding expansions and just over 3,800 in 2017. To search board games listed on *Board Game Geek* by year of publication, conduct an advanced search: https://boardgamegeek.com/advsearch/boardgame. See also Julie Verstraeten, The rise of board games, *Medium* (21 April 2019). Available at: https://medium.com/@Juliev/the-rise-of-board-games-a7074525a3ec.

■ Post a question on *Reddit* or the *Board Game Geek* forums explaining what games you like and asking for suggestions of what to try next. Follow links that say, 'If you liked this game, try these …'

OBSTACLE 4: TIME

'We're all so busy. There just isn't any time. When the kids are free, I still have loads of things I have to do. I can't just stop everything to play games.'

Step 1: clear one hour each week

You don't need to commit loads of time for board gaming to become a regular family activity. Aim to play one game per week as a family. Look at your calendar and find just one hour in the week that you're able to dedicate to playing games. If diaries are busy, just find a time that most of you can make. It is better to play one person down than not to play at all. Give this hour the importance it deserves and make sure everyone knows it is happening in advance.

I realise that playing for just one hour a week won't reclaim your children from the screen. But as the family gets hooked on tabletop gaming the amount of time each person will choose to spend playing will increase. You'll be surprised how much extra time everyone can find when it is something that they all really want to be involved in.

Step 2: embrace the filler

There are plenty of opportunities to sneak games into your daily life, which don't require a clear evening and forward planning. Enter the filler. Fillers are short and usually light games that can be used to plug otherwise dead holes in your day. These games fill the spaces when you might otherwise be hanging around. If you're waiting for one person to get ready to go out, for a friend to arrive, or for dinner to be served in a restaurant, pull out a filler. The moments when you glance around the room and everyone is on a different smartphone or tablet, lost in their own virtual worlds with the TV playing in the background, those moments might be prime opportunities for a filler.

The great thing about a good filler is that it provides a complete and fun game experience with very little commitment needed from the players. If you struggle to get your children to spend more than 20 minutes with you – and then only when they are shovelling food into their mouths – then grab some simple fillers that can be played while you eat. Yes, it may seem as if this is bribery with food, but I'm okay with that. Evening meals provide anchor points at which the family meets.

A short game can give everyone a focus that isn't just on each other. A filler is a prop to help us interact. Instead of fumbling around for topics of conversation, you talk about the game. Silence is no longer awkward; it is concentrated. Fillers can give us precious moments with children who can often seem distant. Your stocks of shared experiences are replenished, providing new topics of conversation for the future.

Just because fillers are quick and easy to teach doesn't mean that they are mindless or dull. In fact, as a hard and fast rule, you *must* avoid games that you find dull. If you find a game boring, the chances are that everyone else will too. You don't want a 20-minute filler to become the longest 20 minutes of the day. Here are some recommendations for simple but 'thinky' fillers to get you started:

- **Red7.** A great card game for 2-4 players in which each player must be in the lead after their go to stay in the game. Fit in a few rounds as each one will only take five minutes.

- **Biblios.** As an abbot of a medieval monastery you are competing with other players to amass the best library of sacred books. Combine strategic planning with decent bluffing to triumph in this 30-minute filler.

- **Kingdomino.** You'll need a little bit more table space for this brilliant game, as each person will build a kingdom around their castle using dominoes displaying different terrain. Very easy to learn, but frustratingly difficult to win consistently.

- **Coloretto.** A simple set collection card game with a twist. Players are each aiming to create sets of colourful chameleon cards, but will lose points if they are forced to pick up too many different colours.

- **Dobble.** Place two circular cards next to each other and aim to be the first player to spot the duplicated image within the cards. If you shout correctly first, the cards are yours. Work through the pack in a five-minute frenzy of intense concentration and loud exclamations.

- **Age of War.** I love this portable dice-rolling game, in which you aim to roll combinations that allow you to claim cards. Get a whole set to prevent your opponents from stealing your cards.

Grab a couple of lightweight games and/or a pack of cards to keep in your bag so that you can pull them out in a coffee shop or pub. You could even squirrel away a filler in your car boot to bring out if you're visiting friends. Stow away a roll and write like **Yahtzee** in the glove compartment, and you'll have an activity for when you are waiting to pick someone up.

Step 3: combine game time with visits from family or friends

A visit from family or friends shouldn't prevent game time from happening; in fact, it should enhance it. You can even keep the identity of the guest hidden from the family to add to the anticipation. Hopefully there won't be too much disappointment when Auntie Susie turns up and they were expecting a minor celebrity to join them. Hosting a visiting gamer or two also changes the dynamic around the table. The family is likely to be better behaved and more attentive to the metagame, providing your guests are well-behaved themselves. If your special guests have favourite games of their own, you can arrange for them to lead a new game. Being a learner alongside your children is a good way of levelling the status at the table.

Step 4: occupy the enthusiastic gamer

After successfully introducing game nights to your family and sparking an interest in, and love of, board games, you may find that there comes a time when your children want to play more games than you do. Don't panic. There are alternatives to sending them back to their games consoles so that you can have a break (or get on with everything else that needs doing). An obvious solution is to encourage subsets of the family to play games without you there, and sometimes this works marvellously. But if your presence is required to keep the metagame functioning or if the wrong game is chosen, you might end up having to get involved so that no blood is shed. In our household, sometimes just one person wants to play. Here are some ideas to keep the lone enthusiast busy:

■ **Elect a game of the month.** The game of the month should be designed for solo play or have a one-player variant. Members of the family each play this game multiple times during the month, making a note of their scores each time. There is no limit to the number of games each person can play. Make a game of the month noticeboard (perhaps on the back of the toilet door) that broadcasts what this month's game is and enables players to post their scores.

■ **Challenge them to learn a new card game** that can subsequently be taught to the family at the next game night or when everyone is ready to play. Books of card games can be bought very cheaply, although the easiest way to learn new games is probably to watch some YouTube tutorials. As well as learning how to play the game, thought needs to be given to how the game should be taught so that its introduction to the family is as smooth as possible.

■ **Create a puzzle folder.** A few carefully chosen and well-differentiated puzzles are more likely to be completed than an impersonal bumper book of puzzles is. Cut out interesting puzzles from books, download them from the internet and print them out or even make them up yourself. Laminate them for multiple use, if you wish. At dinner, ask if anyone has managed to complete any puzzles and which ones they liked best. This will encourage engagement and help you to curate the next batch.

■ **Build an expansion to a favourite game.** Many modern games come with a variety of expansions, which add to and extend the game. *Dominion* has loads of expansions that add new cards; *Carcassonne* and *Catan* expansions add new tiles and special meeples; *7 Wonders* expansions add extra wonders, extra cards and more interaction. Your family can make your own additional cards, resources, rules and tiles to extend your firm favourites.

■ **Play a competitive multiplayer game solo.** My granny always used to play *Scrabble* on her own: her left hand playing against her right. The skill of playing each hand to win and 'forgetting' what your other hand is holding is a brilliant one to develop if you start making your own games and need to do some early testing before you involve others. It is remarkably satisfying to play a big game on your own, as you're never waiting for other people to finish their turns.

- **Play a co-operative as all the characters.** *Pandemic* works really well with a solo player playing multiple hands. The individual can develop strategy and experiment with tactics without having to negotiate with other players.

- **Start a family board game blog or newsletter.** Board gamers' enthusiasm often extends beyond playing games and into writing or talking about them, and possibly even into creating their own. With a family blog, obsessions with board gaming have an outlet. Task your family with making how-to-play videos or game reviews and top ten lists for starters (more on this in Chapter 7).

VICTORY POINTS

- Avoid games that hit your 'emotional buttons' as a family. Pay attention to argument triggers and find work-around solutions for the future.

- Experiment with team playing to improve confidence, collaboration and chances of success, and turn to multiplayer games in which interaction between players is minimal if the mood is tense and explosions are likely.

- Don't demand smartphone-free game playing. Instead, make sure the experience on the table is more interesting than anything happening in the online world. Encourage the family to decide how they want to manage smartphones at the table.

- Sell the games you don't play very often and reinvest the proceeds into your board-gaming budget.

- Maximise your budget by buying second-hand games from online forums, charity shops and conventions, and by downloading free PnP games to satisfy your need for hot new gaming experiences without the price tag.

- Use fillers to snatch time with your children and to normalise tabletop gaming as a family activity.

CHAPTER 7

TAKING BOARD GAMING FURTHER

Expand your game playing.

GAMIFYING LIFE

Games do not need to be restricted to the table. Weave elements of friendly competition throughout other aspects of family life to increase engagement and draw everyone together. Do you have TV programmes that you like to watch as a family? Maybe you are all *Britain's Got Talent* fans or *The Great British Bake Off* is your guilty pleasure. As children get older their feelings about the importance of these family TV shows may change. Maybe the format has got a bit tired for them, maybe sitting round with their parents watching people watching ovens is just not the most interesting thing in their lives any more. In the past, I've been guilty of demanding that my eldest watch *Strictly Come Dancing* with us because, 'We *all* love it', only to find him staring me down during the whole show, his jaw set, and subsequently being reminded by my husband that forcing the children to watch mindless telly isn't what we do. Now, clearly I'm not advocating that family time should always be spent in front of the TV. But if the family is together, watching a programme that everyone enjoys and, crucially, talking and laughing about it, then that is a positive experience. You might vary the programmes you watch together to keep your teens engaged in family viewing, but before you give up on the old favourites, try making a game of it.

Construct a set of Bingo cards, one for each member of the family. Bingo cards can be 3x3 grids, giving each card nine squares. Write down catch-phrases or common occurrences from the TV show in each square on each grid. If you can, give each person a totally different grid. If you need to repeat items, just make sure that no two cards share too many duplicate phrases. Make all the cards before you decide who will get each one. Try to construct them so that each card is pretty evenly balanced, with a combination of more and less likely to occur options. Get the family to help you.

Before the show, randomly distribute the cards. As you watch, players can cross off items from their card as they appear in the show. Your *Strictly* cards might include 'disaster, darling', 'fab-u-lous' and 'a score of 40'. *Bake Off* cards might involve 'a handshake from Paul', 'a soggy bottom' and 'someone mistaking salt for sugar'. For *Britain's Got Talent*, you could have 'the golden buzzer', 'a standing ovation' and 'a contestant saying that this is a dream come true'. Players compete to get the first line, four corners and full house.

Bingo need not be restricted to TV shows. Spice up other family events by constructing a related Bingo game. Kids not too keen on visiting Grandma? Grandma Bingo! ('Don't forget to take your shoes off', 'Who wants a lovely biscuit?' and 'I really must finish that knitting.') Kids moaning about going on a walk? Countryside Bingo! ('Field of sheep', 'horse chestnut tree' and 'MAMIL' (middle aged man in Lycra).) If you have super-competitive children, you might even be able to gamify household chores to encourage them to do the tasks they least like. Issue each child with a Bingo card at the start of the week. When they do a chore, they can check off the corresponding box in their grid. Of course, you can't overuse Bingo as it will lose its appeal and cease to do the job of making a less interesting task more engaging. But Bingo need only be the beginning. Other games can be adapted too.

You could play **Cluedo** in a stately home. Find a map of the house and the rooms that are open to the public before you leave. Do a little bit of research about items that can be found in the house. Give your family **Cluedo**-type names and maybe even suggestions for costumes. Make up sets of cards for the rooms, the items and the players. Remove one card from each set without looking to form the murder cards. Players are given an equal number of the remaining cards. Players can ask each other questions in real-time as they move around the stately home. To ask a question of another player, you must be in the same room as they are. You can only ask about another player if they are in the room too. You can only ask about a room when you are in that room. It is probably best not to move the treasured items around the house as you are likely to be ejected, but players should be able to say where they have seen the item (and possibly give some additional information about it). Players are not party to all the questions asked by the others as they are in the tabletop version. When players are ready to make an accusation, they go to a predetermined place within the house or grounds and wait for the others. Players announce their deductions in the order they arrive at the meeting point. The first to guess correctly wins the game.

During family outings, create a *Scattergories* scavenger hunt to suit your location. When popping into town to do some jobs, categories could include 'brand name', 'mode of transport' and 'sandwiches'. When visiting friends, examples of categories might be 'something found in a kitchen cupboard', 'plant or tree' or 'author'. Players take pictures of examples within the categories that begin with a designated letter of the alphabet. Photos are shared and scored when you get back home (or on the car journey).

Family excursions can also be used to create games that you can play when you return home. While visiting a museum, give your family the task of discovering information that can then be used to construct a Two Truths and One Lie game. Each player must find two pieces of true, but obscure, information about an object or topic. They must then fabricate a third piece of information. Back at home, players share their three pieces of information and the others have to deduce which is the lie. Of course, anyone who has really engaged with the exhibits has a slight upper hand as they may have read information that will help them. Museum visits can also be used to construct your own Top Trumps cards. I don't think it is too controversial to say that the act of constructing the cards is more interesting than playing the game. Or make your own **Wits and Wagers**, with players constructing questions based on the museum visit and other players guessing the answer. The questions need to yield numerical answers – such as a date, distance or quantity. Bet on yourself being the closest or bet on other people's answers and still benefit.

One summer, we didn't have a holiday booked, so I selected ten places, all within a one-hour drive, that I wanted to visit over the six-week break. These were places that I knew the children enjoy, but that I predicted would elicit moans because it was clear that they were educational visits. I wrote all these place names on pieces of paper and put them into an old dishwasher soap carton which I elaborately decorated with the words 'Magical Mystery Tour'. When we had a day free, one of the children would delve into the box to discover where we were going that day. This element of randomness added to the excitement. No explanations were given, just the name, sometimes with appropriate adjectives added – for example, 'Glorious Stansted Mountfitchet'. They didn't know what to expect until we got there. This idea is the brainchild of my husband, Paul. He calls it Tombola Theory and encourages teachers to use it in the classroom to increase engagement.

You need not restrict your ideas to games for the whole family to play. Make up your own games to play by yourself as you do those things in life that might otherwise be boring. My mum, now 81, swims 12 lengths three or four times a week. She gets bored when just counting the lengths so entertains herself by choosing a category – birds or authors perhaps – and thinking of as many things that fit in that category as possible. During each length she works on a different letter. It takes two sessions to go through the alphabet, with X, Y and Z being tackled over just one length. Then the category changes. Mum also used to entertain herself by trying to find car registration plates featuring every number from 1 to 999. This was in the 1970s and 1980s. On one journey she saw a car with a number 2, and then another with a number 3. 'Oh, that's a shame,' she thought, 'it would have been nice to see number 1 first. I'll have to start at the beginning.' Before I was born, she began looking for a car with a number 1. When she found that, she moved on to 2. She always knew what number she was on and looked at number plates every time she drove. She found 999 when I was about 10 years old. She felt relieved rather than accomplished.

DESIGNING YOUR OWN GAMES

If your children claim to prefer board games to video games, if they get upset when a game night has to be cancelled, or if you find yourself playing **Terraforming Mars** for the third night in a row, then your family may be ready to take things a step further. When you get really hooked, board gaming can be a very expensive hobby. With a glut of new games coming to market every year, temptation is unavoidable. When several members of the family are hooked, there will be even more games that go on the wish list. Unless you are prepared to remortgage your house to pay for your new collection, and to build an extension to house it, you'll need to arm yourself with a plan.

Create your own twists on standard games. These twists might start as house rules. If you find yourself wondering what would happen if you adapt certain game mechanics, then try it. Add completely new elements to games or change the victory conditions. To get the ideas flowing, try holding family game adaptation and design competitions. Post a weekly challenge that requires individual family members to think creatively, experiment and then pitch their idea during dinner or prior to game night. Here are some ideas for challenges:

- Create a competitive mode for a co-operative game, or a co-operative mode for a competitive game.
- Create a game that uses the components, but not the board, of a current game to create an entirely new one. Or create a game that uses the board, but none of the components, of a current game.

- Combine two classic games to make a mash-up.
- Make a game expansion that adds new characters with different abilities to an existing game.
- Make a game expansion that adds new power cards or resource types to an existing game.
- Create a solo or two-player variant of a game that starts with a higher player count.
- Alter or adapt a mechanism in an existing game to completely change the outcome and the strategy required to be successful.

Recently my son, Bertie, shared his idea about how to make *Connect 4* 'more epic'. Note that you'll need two *Connect 4* sets for this – one regular set and one that has been customised to allow for the number of players participating in the epic. This will involve painting or putting stickers on some of the counters so that you have a different colour for each player. Two players play a normal game using the regular set. At the end of the game, the winner takes one of their customised counters and places it in the customised set. Players compete in a series of regular games and each time they win they place a counter in the customised set. The first to connect four on the customised set wins the epic. We don't even own *Connect 4*, so I'm not sure what triggered this idea. Granted, it would be more convenient, and cheaper, if he could have ideas that relate to games we actually own.

It is possible to modify or develop most games, even Noughts and Crosses. You may have heard of, or even played, Noughts and Crosses in three dimensions. Here there are 27 possible spaces for you to play in, instead of nine. Visualise a 3x3x3 cube: you can win by getting three in a row on any of the three levels, or you can get a vertical, horizontal or diagonal line across the levels. You can play on normal paper by drawing the three levels next to each other. With a standard 2D game, there are eight possible winning lines, with the 3D version, there are 49 possible winning lines. The game is immediately much more interesting.

When the game design bug sets in, you or others in your family can move from adapting existing games to creating your own from scratch. Designing your own games doesn't have to be as scary as it sounds. Start with small challenges involving light games and work your way up. There are many open board game design competitions that you can use as inspiration for house challenges – or, indeed, you could choose to enter. The 'design contests' forum on *Board Game Geek* is a good place to start. Or you could try the following ideas for starters.

- Design a game that uses one standard pack of playing cards and six dice.

- Design a short game using something un-gamelike that you have around the house – for example, the spices in the spice rack, an old set of toy cars, a keyboard, flowerpots or egg boxes.

- Design a filler game that can be played by two players in under 15 minutes.

- Design a game around a chosen mechanism – for example, bidding, set collection or acting.

- Design a game around a chosen theme – for example, Vikings, moon exploration or rival chocolate tycoons.

- Design a game that is based around a custom deck of a maximum of twelve cards.

- Design a PnP game that you can email to friends and family for them to test.

It would be a mistake to underestimate the impact of the board game design process on personal creativity and skill development. Most other creative projects are centred on literary or artistic creativity – writing stories, composing music, painting, drawing or sculpting, etc. There are fewer pursuits that allow you to develop mathematical and logical creativity. While English and the visual and performing arts rely on the learner's creativity, maths and science usually focus on building knowledge. Learners' experiences in these classroom subjects will probably exclusively centre around accurately reproducing what others have done before them: following directions, completing pre-constructed problems and replicating experiments. For the child who enjoys maths, there is little opportunity within the school curriculum for creativity. But when you design games, you suddenly find a creative application for mathematical knowledge and discovery. Experimenting with probability, frequency, randomisation, combinations and permutations shifts the balance of a game, altering the speed it moves at, the game length and the overall experience. Experimenting with shape and space alters the construction of the game components and how they move and connect. Square tiles throw up different problems to hexagonal tiles. Polyominoes (connected subsets of square lattice tiling, like *Tetris* shapes) enable creative constructions within defined parameters. Calculating and manipulating the advantage that turn order provides is a mathematical challenge.

One of the best things about this sort of mathematical creativity is that games don't work when you just do it theoretically: all games need to be tested to throw up problems. Unless the game is completely luck-based, the players have to make decisions. When you create a game, you need to test it with lots of different people to see what decisions they make and what issues this generates. Designing games is an iterative process. This is hugely important and extremely liberating. You don't need to understand all the maths behind a game idea to go with a hunch about scoring or component frequency, for example. Try it and see how it works. When you begin to play it becomes clear which elements are overpowered and unbalanced. An interest in and understanding of the maths behind the game often comes from experimenting with ideas and making stepped improvements.

Of course, game design also combines this mathematical creativity with a vast array of other skills and knowledge: artistic and graphic design (free-hand and digital), historical and geographical (exploration of theme), technical (component construction), language manipulation (word and story-telling games) and branding and marketing (naming and pitching the game – even if you're only pitching it to the family). It is relatively straightforward to get a short game in a good prototype form using tools that you have at home, and the realisation of a game that you yourself have taken from first concept to completion is hugely rewarding.

FORMING GAME GROUPS AND ATTENDING CONVENTIONS

You don't have to design games in order to delve deeper into the tabletop world. If you enjoy having special guests on game night, why not start your own family-centred games group. Ask your children to invite one or two of their friends, and get them to bring a parent. Just because this isn't an estab-lished activity yet doesn't mean it can't be. When my family have done this, the adults and children alike really value the experience. Play team games with adults versus children or family teams competing against each other. I find that other parents really love having the opportunity to participate alongside their teenagers and get ideas for games to play at home.

If you fancy a full-on immersion into board gaming, attend a convention for the day or weekend. UK Games Expo is the UK's biggest convention and takes place at the NEC in Birmingham at the beginning of June each year: three days of board gaming over three large halls. Visitors can play the latest releases, play demo versions of games that are not yet in production, feed back on prototypes, buy games, borrow games from huge libraries, enter tournaments, listen to talks, watch game-related shows and podcast recordings, take part in special events, find a table to just play at, buy and sell second-hand games, paint miniatures, acquire promo cards and accumulate a larger than necessary set of custom dice. Pop in for an afternoon or bed down for the weekend. It is a blast and well worth a visit. Other smaller conventions are dotted all over the country throughout the year. Smaller conventions have fewer new releases and vendors, but also fewer visitors, which will appeal to some.

STARTING A FAMILY BOARD GAME BLOG

Start your own family board game blog to share your ideas, experiences and opinions with others, or just to keep as your own record. Take a look at one of the 'how to start a blog' guides available online if you need help getting set up.[1] The blog does not need to be run by the adults in the house; an enthusiastic teen or pre-teen can take care of it. Blogs don't require lots of work or maintenance. Not every post needs to be a carefully constructed opinion piece: indeed, none do.

Yes, this is a screen-based activity, but it will support a deeper delve into the offline world of tabletop gaming. A child involved in curating and updating a family blog will at least be engaging in focused, productive screen-based activities. The existence of the blog and the desire to keep it up to date will add motivation to keep playing and creating new family board-gaming experiences. Remember, the goal isn't to eradicate screen time, it is to get a better balance and to reclaim time spent as a family.

Here are some ideas to get the family posting:

■ **Create your own how-to-play videos.** Look at a variety of similar videos online and think about what makes these videos accessible. What do you like about them and what makes you search for another. Think about the length, the camera angle, the introduction, the setting, the quality of the recording and the number of people in the video. Grab a cheap tripod and set up your smartphone camera to record in landscape view. Avoid shooting videos in portrait. Set up two different smartphones if you want to capture different angles. Edit and upload on YouTube or Vimeo. Write up a short overview and embed the video within a blog post.

---

1   Scott Chow has some useful advice: Scott Chow, How to start a blog in 2019, *The Blog Starter* [blog] (10 May 2019). Available at: https://www.theblogstarter.com/.

Write or record your own game reviews. Video, audio and text are all great forms for game reviews, so select the format that works best for you. Develop your own style and structure for reviewing. You might like to give a brief overview before launching into the best and worst bits. You can give a star rating or a score out of ten if you wish. Consider comparing the game to others and saying why it is better or worse, and giving listeners/viewers/readers recommendations that they can try if they like this one.

Record play-throughs. Simpler than explaining how a game works or giving a review, the play-through shows the game in action. These videos help others who are learning the game and developing tactics to see how others play it.

Write top ten (or top five) lists. What are your top ten card games? How does your top ten compare to others in the family? What is the family top ten? Write lists for each of the different genres of games you play: tile placement, abstract, racing, deck builders, bluffing … If you've not played many games, what about your top ten board game components? Or top ten *Munchkin* cards? What about your all-time top ten board games? Top ten lists change over time, but a blog post is a snapshot, showing your top ten at that moment. You can always compile another top ten when you have played more games.

Upload reports from your family game night. This could be a series of photos, a list of events, a brilliantly crafted piece of reportage, interviews with family members or a dissection of the accompanying metagame. You might choose to focus on game highlights, interesting tactics, strange occurrences, winning combinations or unfortunate mishaps.

Share ideas that you've had for new games, new cards, expansions, adaptations and house rules. Share photos of prototypes or just upload an audio of you describing your ideas.

Run polls to allow other people to vote on their favourite games of different types. List five party games, add photos of the boxes and post links to the descriptions on *Board Game Geek*. Allow visitors to add comments to the page after they have voted and ask for suggestions of games that your family should try.

Upload puzzles and treasure hunts that you've completed, participated in or created. If you find a puzzle online that you think is very clever, if the theme appeals or if the mechanics are different from other puzzles you've done before, add a link to it, write an overview or some brief comments about why you like it.

■ **Share links** to events, groups, websites, videos, games, hunts, escape rooms – anything that your family would recommend to other board game families. Bookmark the websites that you find particularly useful or helpful, then when you have a good selection of bookmarked resources, create your own directory of links.

■ **Pose great board-gaming questions** to trigger interesting comments. Questions like:

🎲 What game has had the most impact on you?

🎲 What are your game-playing rituals?

🎲 What is the most unusual game you've ever played?

■ **Create checklists** that will help people to set up their own family game nights, visit a games convention for the first time, introduce new games to friends or pack games for a holiday. What are your top tips for these situations?

■ **Design infographics about board gaming.** Collect some facts about one of your favourite games, game designers or publishers. If the kids are looking for a project, get them to look at the box of their favourite games and learn about the publishers. You could make a pretty interesting (and long) infographic about the work of Reiner Knizia, for example – designer of over 500 games and counting.

■ **Put together a board game quiz.** Test people's memory of board game classics and search out some trivia. Is Coventry Street more expensive than Leicester Square in *Monopoly*? What is the name of the murder victim in *Cluedo*? What colour is the history cheese in *Trivial Pursuit*?

PLAYING WITH BIG GROUPS

For me, one of the best things about meeting up with friends and family is playing games. I have engineered many a family get-together purely for gaming purposes. Oops, rumbled. There are some brilliant games that only work with larger numbers and there are loads more that work well with high player counts. Here are some ideas of where to start when the group is big.

Party games

Party games can be found in most households. These are the mainstream fodder of the board-gaming world. Party games often provoke a Marmite response – you either love them or hate them. Indeed, the word 'party' itself appeals to some but sends shivers down the spines of others, and herein lies the problem. For a party game to be successful with a large group it must appeal to everyone.

Before we get into the good stuff, let's take a moment to look at some of the features of party games, which often put people off and make them run a mile, claiming to 'hate all board games':

- **Being in the spotlight.** Games that require an individual to be on display while others watch; particularly games that involve acting – for example, *Time's Up*, which is based on charades.

- **Pressure to be clever.** Games that reward witty or intelligent responses – for example, Balderdash, in which you make up definitions of words.

- **Fear of the unknown.** Games in which the format changes and the tasks are unpredictable – for example, *The Dangerous Book for Boys Game,* which throws up a mixture of knowledge tasks, skilful activities and mental agility.

- **Bluffing.** Games that require you to lie convincingly or deceive others – for example, *Werewolf*, in which you have to work out who you can trust.

- **Humiliation.** Games that allow players to pick on other players and make them perform tasks against their will – for example, *Bar Pig.*

- **Time pressure.** Performing a task before a buzzer or bell goes off – for example, *Taboo*, a game in which you must describe a word or phrase to your teammates without using any of the banned words.

- **Knowledge isn't power.** Games in which you can be correct without being right – for example, *Outburst!*, which requires you to name the specific words on a card.

- **Noise.** While any party game can get noisy, some are designed to be noisy – for example, *Hullabaloo*, in which players guess what you are doing by the noise you are making.

Awareness of what turns people off games helps us to select games for large groups that will appeal to the greatest number of people. Some people may sit and watch from a safe distance before deciding that it is safe to join in. Don't try to put pressure on anyone to participate as this may cause stress and possibly complete withdrawal.

Telestrations is an extension of the old pencil and paper game picture consequences. Wonderfully simple to teach and often hilariously funny to take part in, this drawing and deduction game gets everyone involved in a low-risk setting without shining a spotlight on any one individual. Each round is super-quick, so members of the group can duck in and out as they wish. Recently, at a family gathering, the seven adults were in the kitchen and the seven children were in the lounge. After a while, we realised that the lounge had gone very quiet; fearing the worst, I poked my head around the door, only to find a self-organised game of *Telestrations* in full swing, with each child concentrating exclusively on creating brilliant artwork. I love a game that doesn't require adult supervision or organisation for success.

A Fake Artist Goes to New York takes the classic party game themes of bluffing, deduction and drawing and combines them in a fabulously inclusive and brilliantly fun way. Everyone draws the same object, one pen stroke at a time. Each player knows what object they are drawing except one, the fake artist. Players try to draw badly or obscurely to throw the fake artist off the scent. The fake artist must stay hidden and deduce what object is being drawn. If you don't mind paying an (unnecessarily) high price for a tiny box, you might really enjoy this one.

In recent years, *Codenames* has catapulted itself to the top of the party game tree and is currently firmly number one in this genre. In the game, players split into two teams, each with an elected spymaster. The spymaster gives one-word clues to help their teammates correctly select words from a tabletop grid without accidentally benefiting their opponents or selecting the assassin. Players make decisions together, providing a collaborative experience. You have to use your brain to think laterally, but the game requires no complex knowledge, so everyone can compete on a level playing field. Teams can be balanced to make the game as fair as possible. Players with more experience can start as spymasters or go on a smaller team.

For a fast-paced card-drafting and set collection game for up to 8 players, try *Sushi Go Party*. Earn points by making sushi combos and customise games for maximum replayability by choosing items from the à la carte menu. This is a very easy to learn but satisfyingly thought-provoking and highly entertaining game. It plays quickly - in about 15–20 minutes - so you can have multiple rounds during a large gathering, with people jumping in or out as they wish; a good party option.

You don't have to opt for a dedicated party game when you have a big group. There are other types of games that work equally well with larger numbers. My favourite genre for big gatherings has to be the roll and write. Every player has an individual board or sheet and chooses how to place centrally rolled dice or centrally revealed cards. Players work in isolation, concentrating on their own boards. I suppose a classic example of this play would be Bingo, although there are no choices to be made in Bingo, it's just pure luck. The other problem with Bingo is that everyone stops as soon as one person has won. For a much more rewarding experience try **Welcome to …** Each player has to build a town. As the architect, you decide which houses get built in what order. You can also build fences, pools and parks which will increase your score. Three cards, each listing a house number and a category, are revealed each turn. Every player makes choices every turn, deciding which card to play and where to place the card within their town. All players have the same board and the same numbers to choose from, but the results on each board will be completely different due to the choices made. Laminate the scorecards so you can use them over and over. You can play solo or with 98 others!

Many social deduction games are best with large numbers. These games rely on individuals holding secret information that others have to discover. You may have to find out which people are on the same side as you, discover a traitor or complete a secret mission. **Two Rooms and a Boom** can be played with up to 30 people. Two teams are split over two rooms, roles are allocated and then a series of three hostage negotiations ensues. At the end of the third round, if the president (on the blue team) is in the same room as the bomber (on the red team), then the red team wins. Otherwise the blue team is triumphant.

Murder games

From party games like Wink-Murder and Murder in the Dark to board games such as **Cluedo**, crime and killing have always been popular themes. You may have tried a murder mystery evening with a group of friends or family. The preparation is fun: becoming the character, fleshing out a back-story, deciding on an accent and a costume. But the evening can fall a bit flat, particularly if some of the players are less than enthu-siastic about acting. Fortunately, there is a much simpler murder-themed game – called, imaginatively, Murder – which works brilliantly with large groups, ideally when they are together over a full weekend.

Get three hats (or saucepans, or flowerpots) and some paper and pens for writing out your categories. In the first hat, put the names of all the players (everyone in the house). Count the number of players. In the second hat, you need to put the same number of places. If you have 12 players, you'll need 12 places. Each place can be a room or another distinct location in the house – for example, the driveway, the garage, the shed … If you don't have enough places for the number of people, you can use each place more than once. Then in the third hat, you need to put the names of objects that can easily be found in the house - for example, a whisk, a tube of toothpaste, a glue stick. Again, you need to have the same number of objects as there are people in the house. Each person now selects a piece of paper from each hat - detailing a person, a place and an object. If they get the paper with their own name on from hat 1, then it must be swapped for another. As soon as the papers are allocated, the game is afoot. Each player has an objective: to get their named person in their named location, holding their named object. For example, if I pick out 'Auntie Alison', 'garden' and 'toilet brush', my aim is to create a situation in which Auntie Alison is standing in the garden holding a toilet brush. When this happens, I would point and gleefully exclaim, 'You're dead!' This eliminates the player you have murdered, in this case Auntie Alison, who should really die a dramatic death on the spot. The murdered player's papers are then passed to the murderer, who takes on the now-dead player's mission as their own. If at any stage a player ends up with their own name as their target, all the remaining players put their character cards back into the hat and redraw.

When playing Murder, there is likely to be a flurry of activity at the start, with children pointedly trying to lead you into the garage and hand you an atlas. Some players may be eliminated in the first 30 minutes. But be prepared for this game to go on in the background all weekend. At some point, the paranoia will set in. Nobody will want to do the drying up in case the person washing the dishes manages to hand them a tube of toothpaste from the suds. Nobody will be prepared to pass the salt at dinner. Nobody will want to help take the picnic things out to the car. Your murder plans need to become more elaborate to trap ever more vigilant family members; your manner more nonchalant. Eliminated players can become accomplices for those who are still in the game, or can form a splinter Murder game when their numbers are sufficient.

Another game that can be played in the background during a large gathering is **_Don't Get Got_**. Each player is secretly allocated a series of tasks that they have to surreptitiously accomplish during the weekend. You may be trying to get another player to sign something, sing a show tune or compliment you on your hair. This game rewards subtle creatives.

Big card games

Card games can also be a winner with huge groups. *Pit* was designed to simulate the experience of being in a noisy corn exchange. Players are dealt nine cards, which display different commodities - for example, corn and wheat. Players take part in a series of blind trades, shouting out the number of cards they wish to trade then exchanging them with an opponent who wants to trade the same number. Collecting a full set of 9 cards allows players to shout out the commodity they have cornered and score the associated points. Some commodities are more valuable than others. It was at a family gathering at a large house in Scotland in the spring of 1998, where I played *Pit* for the first time. It was memorable because of the noise and the torn cards. The table had been abandoned and we were playing on a grand rug in the beautiful drawing room. Everyone started playing sitting down, but fairly quickly the game began to resemble an actual trading floor more and more, with players frantically weaving in between each other to grab passing trades and straining to hear opportunities from the other side of the room. Granny sat in an armchair and relied on the rest of us to come to her, which we did, while stepping over the toddlers. I remember my sister Jenni's jubilant laugh as she shouted 'Wheat!' and pipped my brother to the post.

Another firm family favourite card game is Racing Demon, which I described in Chapter 6. Success completely depends on speed and awareness. There may be scratches, there may be tears, there may even be some cheating, but it may just be one of the most memorable games you play.

Stations

There's one game that has been at the centre of every party and family gathering since I can remember - Stations. Stations can be played in any space - a hall, a field, a garden, a house, a wood - and it can be adapted to suit any theme - wizards, Hollywood, *'Allo 'Allo!*. Stations can be played in teams or as individuals and it can be differentiated and made educational. Energy and luck will triumph over age and strategy. It is a perfect large group party game.

In Stations, a number of cards are posted up in different places around the space before the game is played - and ideally before the players are aware that the game is going ahead. Some may be in full view, others may be hidden a little. These cards should be spaced around, rather than clustered together - use the whole garden or the whole house, or the house *and* garden.

Each card has a list of words or phrases down the left-hand side. After the word or phrase will appear the words 'go to' and then on the right-hand side of the card will be another word or phrase. Every card is completely different.

For example:

Boat	go to	Pigeon
Carrot	go to	Liverpool
Dad's sideburns	go to	Toilet
Maze	go to	**END**

The game play is simple. Every player is given a starting word or phrase - for example, 'carrot' - and a paper and pencil. Then they run off to find that word on the left-hand side of a card. This will, of course, involve finding many other cards too. There will be lots of different starting words, so players will be looking for different things. When they have found their starting word, they look across the row and see the next word that they need to find. In this case, carrot goes to Liverpool. They note down the word Liverpool under carrot on their paper. They now need to look for Liverpool on the left-hand side of another card. Finding the word Liverpool will again give them another word to go to. They may have to return to the same card more than once. Each word they find must be noted down on their paper. At some point they will find the word END. They then have to run back to the gamemaster and show them the list they have written. The gamemaster will check the list against the master list. If it is correct, they have completed the game. If there is a mistake, the gamemaster will send them back to the last correct answer to try again.

If most people are playing individually, but there are one or two who want to play in teams, those people must stay together - they aren't allowed to split up. The best way to ensure this happens is to make them hold hands or to actually tie them together. They will be at a small disadvantage, but it will be funny to watch. If everyone is playing in the same size team, then teams can split up to search for words. Be warned, however, that this will significantly reduce the length of the game. When players have successfully completed their list, they can, should they wish, ask for another starting word to see if they can complete another round before the last of the players completes their first. Or they could collapse on the sofa and ask for a well-earned drink.

The creation of the cards can be complex. It is easy to get into a muddle with the words and find some words that don't go anywhere. However, thanks to my brother Anthony, who decided he needed a more reliable way to create new sets of cards in a speedy fashion, this issue has been solved. He created a spreadsheet that means you can list your themed words in one sheet while, thanks to the nifty lookup function, the cards are auto-populated in other sheets. All you need to do then is print them out. You can download Anthony Wood's Stations Spreadsheet from *The Dark Imp* blog.[2]

The preparation the gamemaster goes through during set-up is duly rewarded. Standing in the middle of the action watching everyone else running past you madly, shooting you looks of delight and exhaustion in equal measure, then eventually running full pelt towards you waving their lists, is something rather wonderful.

If you want to make players work their brains as well as their bodies, then you can develop the game further. As before, there is a list of words or phrases on the left. However, on the right-hand side of the card appears a question. The question must be answered before they can move on, as it is the answer to this question that will appear on the left-hand side of the next card.

For example:

Paris	go to	Which country's flag shows a red circle on a white background?
Nile	go to	What is the capital of Germany?
Victoria	go to	**END**
Swahili	go to	Where would you expect to find fields of tulips?

Anthony's spreadsheet hasn't (yet) extended to this version, so the set-up might take longer, but for some groups, the result will be worth it. Now you

---

2   Ellie Dix, Stations, *The Dark Imp* [blog] (11 March 2019). Available at: https://www.thedarkimp.com/blog/2019/03/11/stations/.

can differentiate routes through the cards so that some starting words take you to easier questions than others. For example, on the geography quiz in this instance, one route might just ask you about European capitals, which would suit a child who is learning about this in school. Another route might require more in-depth knowledge, suiting the resident *Trivial Pursuit* champion. Each person is given a question to start them off, which will lead them to their first answer on the left-hand side of one of the cards.

I created a differentiated Maths Stations game, which I used to play with primary school teachers when I was training them in how to teach maths in a more active way. Teachers had to choose how hard they wanted their questions to be, self-selecting the level of maths they were comfortable with. Most teachers opted for the easiest questions. I've used the same version at my children's birthday parties – shamelessly crowbarring maths into the celebrations. Interestingly, most children opt for the most difficult cards. Maths Stations is also available to download from the same *The Dark Imp* blog post.

Grand tournaments

It is fun to play the occasional game in a really big group. The noise, the energy and the chaos can be electric, and can create game-playing memories that everyone looks back on fondly. But the noise, the energy and the chaos can only be enjoyed for short periods. If you're away for a weekend with a crowd, intersperse your big group game playing with calmer experiences with fewer people.

It is not necessary for everyone to *play* every game for everyone to be *involved* in every game. Use the vastness of the group to engineer structured gaming events that stretch over a period of time and allow a variety of experiences for each individual.

- **Championships.** If you have a favourite or 'house' game that you always play when you are together in smaller groups, then consider running a championship. Give it a grand title if you like – for example, Portsmouth University Boggle Individual Championships (PUBIC). Draw up the structure of the group and knockout stages. Do a grand draw, with all the competitors' names in a hat. Arrange timed competition slots throughout the weekend. Anyone who doesn't want to take part could take on the role of scorekeeper, interviewer or official photographer. A well-prepped championship might even include official T-shirts and a winner's trophy. Co-operative games can also be candidates for championships. Track the players taking part and when the teams are successful. Each player within a team gets a point if the team is successful. The teams are mixed up after every round. The player with the most points after a certain number of games, and therefore the highest win ratio, is crowned champion.

- **Tournaments.** Select a number of games for inclusion in a tournament. The easiest tournaments to organise are those comprising solely of games of the same player count. A group of ten people could have a tournament of two-player games. A group of 24 could play four-player games. Tournaments can be a little tricky to organise, especially if you have an odd number of participants. I created a tournament organiser, which is free to download and might help to make sure that each player plays every game.[3] Players are allocated points according to their standing in each game. These points are then added to the master tournament sheet. Your tournament will have an overall winner, but if you track victory points as well, you can also reward the highest scores within each game.

- **Game stations.** If the idea of organising a full tournament or championship seems unachievable and you don't just want to play games all weekend (who are these people?), then consider setting up game stations instead. Select a number of games that people like and set them up in different locations. Leave a scoresheet next to each game for players to note down when they have played, with whom and the scores they achieved. At the end of the weekend, collect all the scoresheets and crown a winner for each game. Players can choose how many games they play and with whom. They can play the same game multiple times, play each game once, or just play the ones they really like. Players can avoid people they clash with and fit games around the rest of their activities.

- **Team challenges.** Split all the players into teams. Each team should have a team colour, team name and maybe even a team song. Different games are played throughout the weekend on a structured or ad hoc basis. For each game, teams nominate the players who are going to compete for them. This allows keen gamers to play more and less enthusiastic participants to just dip in and out. Points are awarded for each game according to the standings and added to the team leader board. Teams should be a mix of adults and children. Each player can be used according to their strengths, interests and skills. The Golden

---

3 Ellie Dix, Tournament organiser, *The Dark Imp* [blog] (9 March 2019). Available at: https://www.thedarkimp.com/blog/2019/03/08/tournament-organiser/.

Hawks may want Granny to represent them at *Scrabble* but choose to keep her well away from the **Flip Ships** table.

Creating opportunities for a variety of smaller group games within your big family get-together, and mixing up the game-playing partnerships, allows each person to spend time with as many others as possible.

VICTORY POINTS

- Find opportunities to make other areas of family life into a game to create memorable events and further develop your family brand.

- Create expansions or adaptations to games in your collection to get started in game design. Develop your own games using specific parameters to focus your ideas.

- Visit conventions and join game groups to delve deeper into the world of tabletop gaming and find out what is new and hot.

- Create your own family board game blog so members of the family can document your growing immersion in the hobby.

- At big group gatherings, combine big games with tournaments or game stations for smaller subgroups. Structure these events so that people can take part as much or as little as they want.

- Impose a climactic structure on weekends with friends by making all the small games count towards overall standings (and possibly towards a medals ceremony).

CONCLUSION: WHAT NEXT?

Shape your board game family.

You've read the book. Brilliant. Now you need a plan of action. So, write down the practical things you are going to do in the next three weeks. The items on your list should be things that you can absolutely control. For example:

- Find a new PnP game.
- Ask a friend to teach me their favourite card game.
- Find a new place to store and display our family's games.

Got your ideas? Right then, write your list now.

If you'd like a little help in constructing your list, use the Board Game Family Scorecard.[1] The scorecard will help to define your baseline and give you ideas of what to work on first. You can retake the scorecard as many times as you like to track your progress and help you focus on your next steps.

Don't expect your family to instantly transform into your dream board game family. Instead, focus on learning to notice the small successes in engaging your family. I mean really notice them. When you notice a small success, write it down. If your son stops, pauses and watches you play a game over your shoulder for 30 seconds … Success! Write it down. If your daughter makes a positive comment about a board-gaming podcast you're listening to in the car … Success! Write it down.

In three weeks' time, when you've completed all the items on your list, open this book and go through it again to identify your next targets. If you truly intend to make a permanent positive change in your family, you need to keep coming back to the book. There are so many practical strategies, hints and tips packed in here that it isn't possible to implement everything all at once. As your family becomes more engaged, different ideas will become more relevant and will jump out at you when you reread it.

---

1 See https://www.thedarkimp.com/scorecard/.

Read the book. Make a list. Note your successes. Repeat.

After a few spins of the wheel, you'll look back on your previous successes and marvel at how these events, which were once so notable, have become daily occurrences which are woven into the fabric of your family. Looking back and reminding yourself of the distance you've already come will keep you moving incrementally forwards.

It won't take long to make a big change, but it will require your continued effort. To give game playing importance - in order to strengthen relationships in the family - you need to give it high importance in your own life. It will not happen on its own. You are the creator of the new world order in your family: you must carry the torch and keep it high.

Remember, you are way ahead of most other parents. You're leading the pack. You've not only identified a problem, but you're working on a solution. A solution that has the power to do far more than just reduce your family's reliance on screens. Other parents will comment on what great young men and women you're raising. People will ask you for advice and want to know what your secret is. They may look at you strangely when you tell them. They haven't got it yet. But you have. You've got this. You are creating an irresistible offline world that will restore balance, deepen relationships, develop transferrable skills and create shared, long-lasting memories.

Close your eyes and imagine that future.

Now go and get it.

APPENDIX

 Players   Run time   Themes   Mechanics

221b Baker Street

 2-6   90 minutes   Murder mystery   Deduction
Roll and move

In Victorian London the scene is set and there is a mystery to be solved. In this Sherlock Holmes detective game, there are 75 intriguing cases in total. Use your powers of deduction as you travel around the city, collecting clues. Return to Baker Street once you have the correct solution. Careful though, some clues will be cryptic rather than factual, while others may be downright misleading! Obstructing and outwitting opponents as you race to solve the mystery is the aim of the game.

7 Wonders

 3-7   30 minutes  Ancient
civilisation
City building Card drafting
Hand
management
Set collection
Simultaneous
action selection

Played using cards on individual, double-sided boards, the aim is to gather resources, construct buildings, power up your military and develop trade routes as you rule one of the seven great cities of the ancient world. The game is played over three ages in time, using a different deck for each age. It uses the card-drafting mechanism, in which players select one card to play from their hand each turn, then pass the remainder on. Players reveal their chosen cards simultaneously, meaning you can't predict what is going to happen.

7 Wonders Duel

  2 30 minutes  Ancient civilisation City building | Card drafting Set collection

A two-player version of **7 Wonders**, which adapts the game play of the original for one-on-one battles. Take control of your civilisation and decide what to invest in: science, military or prestige. Do you risk attack by spending on technology rather than defence, for example? It's a game of decision making, and there are two new ways to win in this version, which means you have to be even more alert to your opponent's moves.

Acquire

 2-6  90 minutes | Economic Stock holding Tile placement

Players are real-estate tycoons competing over hotel chains. Players found new hotel chains or add to existing ones to gain the chance to purchase stocks within that hotel chain. Hotel chains will merge and while the majority shareholders of the acquired company will receive bonuses, their stock value plummets. Players have to decide when to hold, trade or sell their stocks to secure the best financial advantage. Assets are liquidated at the end of the game and whoever makes the most money from trading stocks and developing their chains wins. This is essentially capitalism: the game.

A Fake Artist Goes to New York

 5-10  20 minutes Party game Bluffing Deduction

Players take it in turns to be the question master, who writes a word on dry-wipe cards and hands them out to the other players. However, one player has been given a card with an X on it, and so doesn't know what the group is trying to draw - they are the fake artist. Using different-coloured pens, they take it in turns to add to a communal drawing that represents the word. Each player has two turns and then it's time to guess who the fake artist is. If the fake artist evades attention, they win. If they are found out, they can still win if they guess the word correctly, meaning the real artists don't want to make the drawing too obvious. This is a creative take on the one-versus-many device.

Age of War

 2-6 15-30 minutes Medieval Press your luck Set collection

Age of War is a conquest game set in feudal Japan. Players compete to conquer as many of the 14 castles as they can, which are represented by cards. Each castle card shows a combination of icons – swords, samurai, crossbows and horses. These icons also appear on the faces of seven dice. Players roll the dice, deciding which to keep and which to re-roll at each stage. The most valuable castles require difficult combinations of icons, so successful attacks are rare. Players must decide how far to push their luck, whether to go for the easy castles, which may be prone to attack from others, or to go all in on the bigger prizes and risk walking away with nothing.

Agricola

 1-5 30-150 minutes Farming Worker placement

Players are farmers trying to scratch out a living for themselves and their spouse. You need to collect materials, build fences, improve the little wooden shack you live in and bring in the harvest. You'll be able to collect animals, which must be housed in fenced enclosures, but will then breed, bringing you additional food. When you've extended your home, you can have children, who become workers that give you extra actions, but they must be fed. A variety of cards are brought into play, which means you have to be thinking about your strategy and adapting to the game play. Sometimes it's a good choice to stick to your plan; sometimes you had better react to what your opponents do.

Altiplano

 2-5 60-120 minutes Andes Trading  Bag building

Altiplano is a bag-building game set in the Andes. Players are in competition to produce goods from dwindling local supplies of natural resources, trade them and find new sources of income. At the start, players are assigned a role tile which determines their access to the resources and goods that they will need. But they can trade at the market, and fortunes will shift throughout the game. It's a game of strategy with several ways to reach the goal. Players will seek to thwart each other's plans while pursuing their own.

Arkham Horror: The Card Game

 1-2 60-120 minutes Adventure Fantasy Horror Co-operative play Role playing

Players are investigators who have to unravel mysteries that are not of this world. Beings are trying to cross the boundary between our world and the next. After setting up their chosen scenario, players work through a series of cards, across which a story unfolds. Players are forced to make a series of difficult decisions, the outcome of which not only affects the immediate game play, but has an impact over the course of the whole campaign.

Arokah

 1 As long as you want Abstract Puzzle Tile placement

A brain-teasing puzzle challenge in which you have to arrange the different-shaped **Arokah** tiles to form patterns. The tiles can tessellate in various ways to form shapes, many of which resemble the sorts of intricate patterns found in nature - for example, in snowflakes. Designed by mathematician Steve C. Brazier, the properties of these shapes and the patterns they make have caught the interest of mathematicians at the University of Cambridge.

Azul

 2-4   30-45 minutes   Abstract strategy Renaissance   Set collection Tile placement

Players are artisans employed by King Manuel I of Portugal to decorate the walls of the Royal Palace of Évora. The name of the game comes from 'azulejos', the Moorish ceramic tiles that have been popular in Portugal since the fifteenth century. Players are aiming for quality, style and minimal waste when drawing their tiles. This will afford them points, as will creating specific patterns. The highest score wins.

Betrayal at House on the Hill

 3-6   60 minutes   Adventure Exploration Horror   Co-operative play Partnerships Role playing Storytelling

Players design their own haunted house, room-by-room, using the cards provided – so the game board is different every time you play. One player is secretly a traitor, and the rest must discover their identity before it's too late. It's a game of suspense and strategy, using the one-versus-many dynamic. The original game comes with 50 different scenarios, and expansions containing more are available.

Biblios

 2-4   30 minutes   Medieval Religious   Auction and bidding Set collection

Players are abbots in a medieval monastery, competing to acquire the best library of holy books and manuscripts, which appear on different cards. You have a limited amount of gold with which to buy your materials and pay your scribes, so you'll need to be cunning when buying and selling your works. Whoever gains the most victory points wins, but the values keep changing, so you might get more or less than you bargained on. It involves a lot of strategic planning and a bit of luck.

Camel Up

 2-8 20-30 minutes Racing  Betting and wagering
Roll and move

Players place bets on a camel race around an Egyptian pyramid. The camels' movements are determined by the dice that come out of the pyramid shaker, so there is an element of luck, but you'll also need to hold your nerve and judge when to place your bet. The aim is to win the most money. It is a simple but exciting game that is good for families.

Captain Sonar

 2-8 45-60 minutes Nautical Deduction
Grid movement
Partnerships
Real-time
Simultaneous
action selection

In a dystopian future an underwater economic war is being fought. Players are on opposing teams, each manning a next-generation submarine proto-type and trying to protect their underwater mines. Co-operation and teamwork are critical as you try to find and destroy your opponents' subma-rine without being caught yourself. The captain of each team controls the movement of the submarine, which he or she marks on a grid representing the seascape and calls out each movement to all players. The engineer deals with system failures and the first mate powers up the submarine sonar and missiles. But beware, the radio operator on the enemy sub is also listening in and may pinpoint your location. A lack of communication and strategic planning could mean you are sunk!

Carcassonne

 2-5   30-45 minutes   City building Medieval   Area control Tile placement

Players lay tiles to create a landscape – the tiles are a bit like straight-sided jigsaw pieces and have to go together to make up a coherent bigger picture, so, for example, roads have to connect to roads, a city tile can't be placed in the middle of a field, etc. Players can then place their meeples on the tiles to claim an area that is under construction. Once the area is complete, the player gets a point. Deciding where and when to play your meeples is key. Highest score wins.

Cash 'n Guns

 4-8   30 minutes   Mafia   Bluffing Simultaneous action selection

Players are a gang of criminals who are trying to divide up their loot, but no one wants to share nicely. Stick to your guns to try to maximise your share of the cash. The game play involves cards and foam guns. Loot cards indicate the different types and values of the goods on offer, and if an opponent deals you a 'bang' card, you've been shot and are out of the round. Anyone left standing at the end of the round gets to take it in turns to choose a loot card. Richest gangster wins. Bluffing and power play is inevitable.

Catacombs

 2-5   60-90 minutes   Fantasy   Dexterity Role playing

Catacombs is an award-winning fantasy board game. Using the one-versus-many device, one player controls the overseer of the catacomb, who directs the monsters that inhabit it. The remaining players work co-operatively to try to defeat the enemy. They must each use their special abilities effectively if they are to prevail as a team. Players flick wooden discs representing missiles and fireballs at the other characters, so success in the game relies on aim and dexterity as well as co-operative strategy.

Catan

 3-4   60-120 minutes   Colonies  Route/network building
Trading

Players compete to build settlements on the uncharted island of Catan. The objective is to collect resource cards - representing things like stone, wood, grain and sheep - and use these to build up a civilisation. The game is played on a board made of hexagonal tiles - each representing a site of resource production, or the barren desert - surrounded by water. You can arrange the board differently each time, and rolls of the dice determine what resources the island produces, so the game is a bit different on every play. Players can trade resources among themselves or exchange them at ports as they try to achieve their goals. Points are awarded for building up settlements, and the first to 10 points wins.

Catan: Seafarers

 3-4   90 minutes   Nautical
Colonies   Route/network building
Trading

This is an expansion of the classic **Catan** game and so uses the same mechanics. In this version, players are exploring new seas and new lands, seeking to create new sea lanes and settle as-yet-undiscovered islands. It's a game of strategy with a dash of luck. There are several different editions of the **Catan** games, so always remember to check whether an expansion pack is compatible with the version of the game that you have before you buy.

Century Spice Road

 2-5 30-45 minutes Medieval Card drafting
Deck building
Hand
management
Set collection

Players lead a caravan of camels on a trek to establish new trading routes and discover and trade exotic spices, collecting victory point cards as they go. Once the last player has claimed a fifth victory card, the last round is triggered and the player with the most victory points at the end wins. Strategic decision-making is important. The game is themed on medieval traders' travels along the ancient Silk Road and the detailed artwork is by internationally renowned artist Fernanda Suárez.

Citadels

 2-8 30-60 minutes City building
Medieval Bluffing
Card drafting
Set collection

A card-drafting game in which players are competing to create the best city, the aim is to accrue gold to pay for your buildings and so win points. The player with the most points wins. The different characters, and their special abilities, keep things interesting and unpredictable. Some plotting, scheming and deception is inevitable. Expect some conflict.

Claim

 2 25 minutes  Fantasy Trick-taking

Players are competing to gain control of the land after the death of the king. He had no heirs and now power is up for grabs. The objective is to win over followers in phase one, and then, in phase two, to use these followers to win over the five rival factions in the realm. Win over the majority of the factions to win the game. The factions have different powers that affect play and keep things interesting.

Cluedo

 3-6   45 minutes   Murder mystery   Deduction
Memory
Roll and move

Dr Black has been found dead in his own mansion, the victim of foul play. There are six suspects and multiple potential crime scenes and weapons. One suspect, one location and one weapon card are randomly selected and placed in an envelope before the game begins. Players use questioning and deduction to figure out what is missing from play and so solve the crime in this classic whodunnit.

Codenames

 2-8   15 minutes   Spies/secret
agents
Word game   Deduction
Memory
Partnerships
Press your luck

Two teams compete to track down their own secret agents, without revealing secret agents belonging to their opponents and, crucially, avoiding the assassin. A tableau of 25 cards, arranged in a 5x5 grid, is laid out in view of all players. Each team elects a spymaster. The spymaster knows which cards represent their team's secret agents and must offer single-word clues that link as many of these cards together as possible. The team then deduces which cards the spymaster was referring to and makes their guess. Will they find their own people or mistakenly uncover enemy secret agents, innocent bystanders or the deadly assassin?

Coloretto

 2-5   30 minutes   Animals   Card drafting
Press your luck
Set collection

The aim is to collect sets of colourful cards featuring pictures of chameleons. Game play involves drawing cards from the central supply to add to the rows of cards that are laid out, or taking a row to add to the player's own collection. You score points for each card you have of a certain colour, but if you have more than three different colours, you will lose points. Rounds come to an end when the cards run out, and the highest score wins. Be careful to check the specifications if buying online as the game was originally published in German.

Cottage Garden

 1–4   45–60 minutes   Farming   Tile placement

A tile placement game played using individual garden boards, which feature a scoring grid. Points are awarded for planting (placing tiles) in certain areas and for creating patterns. Players collect flower bed tiles from the central market and use these to design their gardens. When one garden is finished, the score is recorded, the flower bed tiles are returned to the market and the player moves on to their next design. Players make five laps of the market before the game enters its last round. The winner is the gardener with the most points.

Cryptid

 3–5   30–50 minutes   Fantasy   Deduction

Players are cryptozoologists who are competing to find the elusive creature that is the Cryptid. Each player has only partial information and needs to glean clues from their opponents, without giving too much away themselves, in order to solve the mystery and win. It's a deduction game that uses a fair amount of misdirection. There are two difficulty levels, five clue books and a deck of over a hundred set-up cards, meaning the variations in the game are almost endless.

Dead of Winter

 2-5　 60-120 minutes　 Zombie Apocalypse　 Bluffing
Co-operative play
Deduction
Storytelling
Voting

Players are part of a small colony of people who have survived an apocalyptic event that has either killed the rest of humanity or turned them into flesh-eating monsters. This is a survival game based in a bleak dystopian future. Each player leads a small faction of survivors, working together but also trying to complete their secret objective, which might sometimes be to the detriment of the group. Crossroads cards introduce situations that the players must vote about. The outcome with the most votes is put into action. The different victory conditions mean that there could be more than one winner, or no winners at all.

Decktet

 Variable　 Variable　Print and play　 Game system

There are dozens of different games you can play with **The Decktet**, which is a deck of custom cards. Like regular playing cards, **The Decktet** has suits, but there are six of them, each containing 10 cards, many of which are double-suited. Additional cards are used in some games but not in others. **The Decktet** is available as a print and play (PnP) game for free, but you can also purchase sets. Download or buy here: https://www.decktet.com/getit.php.

Diamonds

 2-6　 20-30 minutes　 Abstract　 Hand management
Trick-taking

Diamonds is a trick-taking card game with an added tactile point-scoring dimension. Players are aiming to collect diamond crystals, which are worth points. If you cannot follow suit during a hand of cards, you get penalised; if you win a trick, you get an advantage. Players are trying to move diamonds from the supply into their vault, where they are safe from opponents and worth two points. Diamonds in a player's showroom are vulnerable to theft but are worth one point. The player with the most points at the end wins.

Dice City

 1–4   45–60 minutes   City building Medieval   Worker placement

The capital city of Rolldovia has been destroyed and the queen has decreed that a new one will be built. Players take on the role of influential landed nobles and compete to establish their province as the prime location for the new capital city. Managing your resources successfully is important, but the roll of the dice brings an element of luck. Each player has their own game board and set of different-coloured dice. They build their cities by collecting resource cards.

Dobble

 2–8   15 minutes    Abstract   Pattern recognition Real-time

Dobble is a fast-paced game of pattern recognition and reflexes. Players are racing to find the one symbol that two cards have in common. Each card is covered in a multitude of symbols, but each of them will not reoccur more than twice in the deck. Players will need a keen eye for detail, as the size and positioning of the symbols varies too, making the match harder to spot. It's suitable for ages six and over and is a good family game for adults and children.

Dominion

 2–4   30 minutes    Medieval   Deck building

Players are feuding medieval monarchs, each seeking to expand their kingdom and influence. This is a deck-building game, and players are seeking to accrue the most valuable set of cards. They each start with the same deck of ten basic cards, which they shuffle and then draw the top five to form their hand. Luck and strategy both play a part. Game play ends when the communal stock of supply cards has run out. Then the player with the most victory points wins.

Don't Get Got

 2-8   1-2 days   Party game   Acting
Bluffing

This is a covert party game which is designed to run in the background of a social gathering. Players have to keep their guard up as they are each on a secret mission and don't know what the others are planning. There are over 180 different mission cards; players are each given six to pursue, and this will involve tricking one of the other players in some way. If a player sees through your scheme and identifies what you are trying to get them to do, you've lost that mission. The first to complete three missions is the winner.

Exit the Game: The Abandoned Cabin

 1-6   60-120 minutes   Escape   Co-operative play
Deduction
Real-time

Players wake up to find themselves locked in the abandoned cabin in which they took shelter after their car broke down when they were driving along a quiet road through the woods. The windows are barred and the only means of escape is figuring out the code to the combination lock on the door. This is a game of deduction, creativity, problem-solving and teamwork. The game can only be played through once because you have to mark up the board and components as you play.

Fireball Island: The Curse of Vul-Kar

 2-4   45-60 minutes   Adventure   Area movement
Dexterity
Set collection

This is a restored version of the 1980s' classic, *Fireball Island*. The board is a model of the island, which players move their meeples around by playing cards. The aim is to collect the most treasure and to capture the most snapshots (both also represented by cards) before heading back to the helicopter and escaping the island. Players will have to beware the fireballs (marbles) that could come careening down the course at any moment, threatening to derail their game play. It's a fun and lively family game, using set collection strategy and also a bit of luck.

Five Tribes

 2-4   40-80 minutes   Arabian   Area control
Card drafting
Set collection

This is an area control game based in an ancient mythical land: the fabled Sultanate of Naqala. Following the death of the sultan, players are competing to gain influence, conquer the land and become the new ruler. The five different tribes of meeples are arranged on the board before the game begins, and the players are aiming to manoeuvre them to score points and achieve ultimate victory. There are many different pathways to victory, so a considered strategy is essential.

Flip Ships

 1-4   30-40 minutes   Science fiction   Co-operative play
Dexterity

Players are fighter pilots who are trying to defend their planet from attack from the skies. The aim is to flip your ships (cardboard counters) at the enemy planes and to take down the powerful mother ship. If a counter lands on a card that represents an enemy, it does damage. The cards specify how many hits it will take to destroy them. Players are each assigned ships with different special powers but have to work together to defeat the enemy. Dexterity and aim are critical.

For Sale

 3-6   30 minutes    Economic   Auction and bidding

Hand management

Players bid for and buy property in the first round of the game, and then sell it for the greatest profit in the second. The game is played using property cards – there are lots of different types of property, ranging from a cardboard box to palaces and a space station, each with a different face value – and cash tokens which players use as currency. It's a fast and fun game.

Gizmos

 2-4   40-50 minutes   Science fiction   Card drafting

Players are inventors who are competing at the Great Science Fair. The aim is to build the best machine and collect the most victory points. The game uses cards and an innovative 3D marble dispenser – with the marbles representing the energy needed to build and power the machines. The aim is to acquire cards, each representing a gizmo that can be added to the players' machines. One gizmo may trigger another, creating powerful combined actions and earning additional points. The trick is to plan how your gizmos can work in sequence.

Gravity Maze

 1   As long as you want   Abstract   Puzzle

A problem-solving challenge in which the player uses plastic components to build maze-like towers with the aim of getting a marble from point A to point B. There are 60 different challenge cards, which will test your spatial reasoning skills – challenges are given a difficulty ranking, making the game suitable for all ability levels. You could take it in turns to attempt a challenge, and keep score of how many each player achieves, thus turning this one-player game into a multi-player competition.

Grease Monkey Garage

 1–5   30–45 minutes   Print and play Transportation   Worker placement

Players are shift managers in a garage. They need to strategise and plan how to use the shop's limited resources to fix as many cars as they can, directing the mechanics and building a stash of spare parts to enable them to do so. Players earn reputation points for fixing customers' cars, and the player with the most points wins.

Hanabi

 2–5   25 minutes    Abstract   Co-operative play Deduction Memory Set collection

A co-operative deduction game in which players are organising an amazing fireworks display, the name 'Hanabi' comes from the Japanese for 'fireworks'. The game is played using cards, which the players are aiming to group by colour and place in numerical order. Sound easy? Well, players are not allowed to look at their own cards and are reliant on information from the other players to inform their actions. Teamwork is essential in this players-versus-game set-up.

Havana

 2-4   30-45 minutes   City building   Hand management
Set collection
Simultaneous action selection

Players are working to rebuild the Cuban capital city after the Revolution. You gain victory points by constructing buildings, but you have to use your resources to plan and pay for their construction (each building requires a different combination of money, workers and building materials, detailed on the tiles that represent these). More elaborate buildings cost more, but yield more victory points. It's a strategic resource management game with a twist. On each turn the players chose two cards from the 13 in their hand, and the various combinations determine how the round will go. The game calls for forward planning, adaptation and reaction.

Hive

 2   20 minutes   Abstract   Tile placement

A strategic two-player tile placement game, **Hive** is made up of 22 hexagonal tiles – 11 black and 11 white – which each represent different insects that can be moved in different ways. There is no board and no set-up phase; the tiles are simply placed down next to each other. Players are aiming to protect their queen bee while attacking their opponent's – the first to surround their opponent's queen wins.

Jungle Speed

 2-8   10 minutes   Abstract   Dexterity

Players are competing to get rid of their cards first. Everyone plays a card from their hand one by one, and whenever a matching pair comes up, the race is on to grab the wooden totem, which is placed in the middle of play. Whoever gets the totem can hand over their cards to the other players. Success relies on pattern recognition and speed. Some of the patterns are only subtly different, so you have to be careful not to be over-eager and go for the totem when there is no match. This is a lively and fast-paced game.

Junk Art

 2-6   30 minutes   Art   Dexterity

Players use a communal stack of wooden pieces to build their junk art sculptures. There are ten different game modes to choose from. The game uses the card-drafting mechanism to determine which pieces of junk are used (the cards depict the pieces and players pass on cards from their hand before deciding what to play). Once the cards have run out, the player with the tallest work of art wins.

Khet

 2  20 minutes   Abstract Electronic   Grid movement

Imagine an Egyptian-themed adaptation of Chess that uses lasers and you are not far off *Khet*. Players take turns to move their pieces, with the aim of protecting their pharaoh and attacking their opponent's – much like how you'd use pawns in Chess. The pieces are different geometric shapes, and some have one mirrored side, some have two, while others have none. The sphinx pieces contain a laser diode, which can be fired off the mirrors and directed towards the opposing pharaoh. If the laser hits a non-mirrored surface, the piece is removed from play. Hit the opposing pharaoh, and you win. An understanding of geometry and angles is useful.

Kingdomino

 2-4 15–20 minutes Territory building  Tile drafting Tile placement

A tile placement game in which players are competing to build the best kingdom. The dominoes have a number on the back and an illustration of two different types of terrain on the front. Just as the numbers have to match up in dominoes, the picture tiles have to follow on from the ones already in play. Some tiles feature pictures of crowns, which equate to prestige points. The mechanism of allocating tiles keeps things interesting. If you chose the highest number in one turn, you will have to take the lowest number in the next – meaning one player cannot take all the highest value tiles. The round is over when each player has constructed a 5x5 grid. At the end of the game, the scores are calculated by multiplying the size of the terrain by the number of crowns in it: the highest score wins.

King of Tokyo

 2-6 30 minutes Science fiction Area control Press your luck

Players are monsters who are competing for dominance and power in a Tokyo that is overrun by a hoard of unwanted invaders. The roll of the dice determines whether the monsters can gain victory points, build up their energy, go on the attack or heal themselves from damage. Players select which dice to fix and which to re-roll, pushing their luck and testing their nerve. It's a game of strategy with a luck component. The first to 20 victory points, or the last monster standing, wins.

Legacy of Dragonholt

 1-6   60 minutes to as long as you want   Adventure Exploration Fantasy   Co-operative play Role playing Storytelling

Players are working together to complete six different quests in this narrative role-playing game. The game allows players to create their own characters, with different special abilities and attributes. Creating a complementary group of heroes will be key to defeating the game, as will teamwork. Players enter into a fantastical and ever-changing world, in which their decisions will have a lasting impact in subsequent quests. Everything they do is adding to the story. It's a very involved game, so you might want to set aside ample time to play this one.

Magic: The Gathering

 2   20 minutes   Fantasy Fighting   Collectible card game Hand management

Players are wizards who are competing to destroy their opponents in this classic collectible card game (CCG). Players use a deck of cards to duel their rival wizard. Cards represent different things, including creatures, enchantments, lands and artefacts. Wizards play combinations of cards to deal damage to their opponent's creatures or to the opponent themselves. A substantial part of the strategy (and the attraction) is in building the deck to start with, as there are nearly 20,000 cards to choose from. Cards are categorised by how rare they are, and very serious collectors will pay a lot of money for the rarest cards. But, don't panic, you can purchase starter decks, which come pre-made and are reasonably priced.

Mayfly

 2-4   15-20 minutes   Animals   Co-operative play
Deck building

Players are working co-operatively to aid the survival of a mayfly, which will die if it is left without their support. First, the objective is to ensure the mayfly gets enough food. Next, to ensure it does not get eaten by predators while trying to find a partner.

Mechs vs. Minions

 2-4   60-90 minutes   Fantasy
Fighting   Action/movement programming
Card drafting
Co-operative play

Players are mechs from the world of Runeterra, who find themselves working together to fight against an army of minions. There are ten missions in total, and each is a story-driven campaign. The game features modular boards, which allow players to set up the multiple different scenarios. Teamwork and strategy will be essential to success.

Meeple Circus

 2-5   45 minutes   Animals
Circus   Card drafting
Dexterity

Players are competing to create the best circus act by piling up their meeples into the arrangements that the audience wants to see. The aim is to score the most points on the clap-o-meter. You'll need dexterity and a bit of strategy, as before the performance begins, you'll need to hire the best circus acts. This is a good family game. It's meant to be played along to a music track, to time the rounds and set the mood - available via a web browser or smartphone app - so you will need some technology to hand in order to enjoy the full experience of this game.

Mexican Train

 1-8   20 minutes   Abstract
Trains    Tile placement

This can be played with a standard set of double 12 dominoes, although there are branded commercial versions available which have additional themed elements. The aim is to be the first player to get rid of their dominoes, by playing them to create their own train, or by adding them to the group's Mexican Train. There are also ways to block other players' progress, so everyone will need to keep their wits about them. A comprehensive overview of the rules can be found here: https://www.mastersofgames.com/rules/mexican-train-dominoes-rules.htm.

Munchkin

 3-6   30 minutes   Fantasy
Fighting   Card drafting
Hand
management

Players compete to kill monsters and steal magic items in this fast-paced playful card game. Show no loyalty to your fellow players, as this game rewards backstabbing and treachery. Each time a player kills a monster, they go up a level. The first to reach level ten wins.

Nyet!

 2-5   30 minutes    Abstract   Hand
management
Trick-taking

Players are competing to win tricks, but first they need to establish the rules for the round. They take it in turns to eliminate various options regarding the starting player, trumps, value of tricks, etc. until there is just one left in each category. This keeps the game interesting, as the rules are changing each round. Players decide how many rounds they will be playing to before the game begins, and the highest score at the end wins.

Paiko

 2   35 minutes   Abstract   Area control
Tile placement

The game board is divided into different sections and points are awarded if players are able to place their tiles in specific areas. The first to 10 points wins. It's a game of strategy in which players are trying to thwart their opponent's as well as pursue their own. The game is available to download from the creators' website as a print and play (PnP) game: http://paikogame.com/.

Pandemic

 2–4   45 minutes   Medical   Co-operative play
Point to point
movement
Set collection

Players are working as a team to prevent the spread of a deadly disease. Each player takes on the role of a specialist with special infection-fighting abilities. Players move around the map on established routes between cities to treat infection and cure diseases. First published in 2007, the game has proved a hit with novice and expert gamers alike, and has spawned a series of expansions and other spin-off stand-alone titles.

Pandemic Legacy: Season 1

 2–4   60 minutes   Medical   Co-operative play
Legacy   Hand
management
Point to point
movement
Set collection

The game follows the same basic principles as **Pandemic** – players are working to fight the spread of a disease and avert disaster – but this time the virus is unlike anything you have seen before. The game can only be played through once, as you will open sealed envelopes to reveal secret information as the game progresses. All your decisions will have an impact on future game play.

Photosynthesis

 2-4 30-60 minutes Environmental Action point allowance system

Players plant trees which capture energy from the sun, which passes around the board once each round. Any trees that are in the shadow of others will not benefit. This sunlight is used as currency to grow existing trees and plant new ones. Players use their light points to take different actions. They can take as many actions as they wish, provided they have enough light points to pay for them, or they can save their points to use in a future round. Points can be spent on planting seeds, growing trees into bigger trees, making bigger trees available or harvesting trees to gather victory points. The game ends after three rotations of the sun, and the winner is the player with the most points. Points are gained by cutting down mature trees that have come to the end of their lifecycle. But a key part of the strategy is deciding when to cut them down, as while they are in play, they could be casting shadows and preventing your opponents from getting sunlight.

Pictionary

 3-16 90 minutes Party game Drawing Partnerships Roll and move

One player draws a representation of what's on their card, and the others guess what it is. In the branded versions of the game, players roll the die to move along the board, and the first to the finish wins. Newer editions of the game include dry-wipe boards and an updated pop culture category. Of course, you could play your own version by writing clues on scraps of paper and competing to be the first to ten correct answers, for example.

PitchCar

 2-8 30 minutes  Racing Dexterity

This is a very tactile game in which players build the track and then flick their racing car around it. The first to the finish wins, but be careful because if you flick your token off the track, you have to start again. Dexterity and technique are essential. You'll need a lot of space to play this game, as the track components are quite large. It's recommended for ages six and up, so it's a good one for all the family.

Pokémon Trading Card Game

 2 20 minutes Fantasy
Fighting Card drafting
Collectible card
game

This is a collectible card game themed on the popular Pokémon franchise. There are many different Pokémon to collect, each with different powers and abilities. First, players build their decks, which will include their Pokémon and also trainer and energy cards, which affect the game in different ways. Players are competing to be the first to defeat six of their rival's characters.

Power Grid

 2-6 120 minutes Economic
Industry Auction and
bidding
Network building

Players are power plant owners who are competing for the monopoly in supplying cities. They have to acquire the raw materials to make the energy – except in the case of the valuable renewable commodities. Players need to strategically balance their income and outgoings, while trying to maximise the efficiency of their production methods and expand their networks. The turn-taking mechanisms keep power in check by forcing players who are getting too far ahead into weaker positions in the bidding and purchasing order.

Railroad Ink

 1-6   20-30 minutes   Trains   Roll and write Route/network building

Players work on individual dry-wipe boards to plot the best network of roads and railways. The aim is to connect as many exits as possible, in order to score points. But points are lost for starting routes that you can't finish, so careful planning and strategic thinking is a must. The rewards for risk-taking are great, but so are the punishments when it doesn't pay off. Highest score wins. There are two different versions of the game: in the Deep Blue Edition, players can extend their networks over the water; in the Blazing Red Edition, players have to beware the volcanoes that can suddenly erupt and the meteors that may fall and threaten their best-laid plans.

Railway Rivals

 2-6   90 minutes   Racing Trains   Roll and move Route/network building

Players are competing to build the most profitable railway routes by joining together cities on the dry-wipe board, and then to race trains between two places that are chosen at random. The winner and runner-up of the races win prize money, which they can then invest in their network. It costs more in-game currency to build over mountains, for example, but the pay-off is a shorter route. The winner is the player with most money in the bank at the end.

Red7

 2-4   5-30 minutes   Abstract    Hand management
Set collection

The game uses a deck of 49 cards, in the colours of the rainbow and numbered from 1 to 7. Each card has a winning condition listed on it, and the card at the top of the discard pile determines what players need to do to win that hand. Simply, you need to win on your turn, or you are eliminated from play. The winner is the last player remaining.

Risk

 2-6   120 minutes   War game   Area control
Dice rolling
Set collection

Players have the rather grand ambition of taking over the world in this game of conquest, diplomacy and control. The board is a map of the world, and players move their model armies to conquer and control their territories. Alliances are made and broken, and game play can take quite some time. Players are aiming to conquer the most territories in order to win.

Rolling Ranch

 2-20   10-20 minutes   Animals   Roll and write

Players are competing to rebuild their ranch after a hurricane. The aim is to rescue escaped animals, rebuild the farm buildings and construct new ones. Everyone plays at the same time on their own ranch sheet, recording their choices as they go along. The game ends when someone has filled in their sheet, and the player with the most points (gained from meeting their objectives) wins.

Room 25

 1-6 30 minutes Science fiction Action programming
Bluffing
Co-operative play
Deduction
Partnerships
Simultaneous action selection

Players are trapped in a prison and must find Room 25, the rumoured exit from this nightmare entrapment in which all the rooms have four doors but seemingly no real exit. Each turn, players select their movements and lock them into a programme, which is revealed as the turn plays out. The objective is to escape from this hellish maze, but not everyone is working for the same goal. Some players are secretly given the role of guardians, who will betray the group if they get the chance. It's a co-operative game with a one-versus-many twist.

Root

 2-4 60-90 minutes Animals
Fantasy
War game Area control
Variable player powers

In this asymmetric fantasy board game, players take on the role of different factions who want to assume rule of the forest kingdom. As each faction has a completely different style of play and victory conditions, you can play again and again without exhausting all the possibilities – it is the interaction between the players that really shapes the game.

Rummikub

 2-4  60 minutes Abstract
Number Set collection

Players are competing to be the first to get rid of all their numbered tiles, which they do by making groups (tiles of the same number value but a different colour) or runs (consecutive numbers of the same colour) of three or more tiles. Players can add to and rearrange sets that are already on the table. It's rather like the card game Rummy, but with tiles instead of cards and colours instead of suits.

Rush Hour

 1   As long as you want   Abstract   Puzzle

Players are aiming to free the red car from a traffic jam in this tactile 3D logic puzzle. The game comes with cards which illustrate different ways of setting up the board and the blocking cars and trucks. Vehicles can only slide up and down and left to right, and the puzzles are graded by difficulty. It's a great game for developing logical reasoning and critical thinking skills.

Santorini

 2-4   20 minutes   Ancient Mythology   Tile placement

Players are aiming to move their meeples to the third storey of the building they are constructing in this accessible strategy game. On each turn, they can move one space, and then lay down one building block. The board and building materials are 3D and are modelled on the white and blue towering houses that are common in Santorini, hence the name of the game. Following the ancient Greek theme, the game uses God cards, which allow players to bend the rules.

Scotland Yard

 3-6   45 minutes   Police Travel   Deduction Partnerships Point to point movement

This is an asymmetric, one-versus-many game in which one player is Mr X and the rest are the detectives who are working together to try to catch him.

The board is a map of London, and players are moving around using various modes of transport. The police know what type of transport Mr X is using, but have to deduce his exact location. The detectives win if one of them lands on the same square as Mr X, and Mr X wins if he can evade capture until the detectives have run out of transport tokens and can't make any more moves.

Shakespeare

 3-6   20-90 minutes   Renaissance   Card drafting

Players are theatre managers who are competing to put on the best production and win the patronage of the queen. They have six days to hire the best actors, source all the props and costumes they will need and rehearse the play. Players use individual game boards but are competing for the same resources from a central supply. Certain actions win or lose you prestige points, and the highest score at the end wins.

Small World

 2-5   40-80 minutes   Fantasy Fighting   Area control Dice rolling

Players are competing for control of a miniature fantasy world that's not big enough to accommodate all of them. It's a territory expansion game, in which players use their troops - which are comprised of different fantasy characters, like dwarves, wizards and giants, each with different special abilities - to try to push their opponents off the face of the earth. Points are scored based on how many territories your empire covers, and the highest score wins.

Solenia

 1-4   30-45 minutes   Exploration   Hand management

Solenia is a planet which has stopped rotating, leaving the north plunged in permanent darkness and the south in constant sunlight. Inhabitants of the planet have survived by building up transport networks and trading goods. Players are controllers of the airships that are needed to deliver vital goods to the floating cities in both the light and dark realms. Players start with 16 cards, and have to play one each round, with the aim of racking up the most gold stars - highest scorer wins.

Space Alert

 1-5   30 minutes   Science fiction Space exploration   Action/movement programming Co-operative play Real-time Simultaneous action selection

Players work together as a crew of astronauts to beat the game in this deep space adventure. They are on a mission to survey an unexplored, and potentially dangerous, part of the galaxy and must protect the spaceship for the ten minutes it will take to map out their surroundings. Challenges are graded by difficulty, and it will take teamwork and strategy to master them. The game comes with a soundtrack, which sets the mood and acts as a timer, so you'll need a CD player handy to get the full experience.

Space Cadets: Dice Duel

 4-8   30 minutes   Fighting Science fiction Space exploration   Action/movement programming Partnerships Real-time

Each player mans a station on a spaceship and the captain of each team oversees and coordinates their actions as they go into battle with their opposition. There is no formal turn-taking, and everyone just makes their moves as quickly as they can. The action is fast-paced and lively. The game ends when one side is destroyed.

Splendor

 2-4   30 minutes   Economic Renaissance   Card drafting Set collection

Players are gem merchants who are competing to acquire mines, shops and means of transportation, and to attract the patronage of the nobility in this medieval-themed contest. The aim is to reach 15 prestige points, and the first to hit that total wins. The game is played using cards and tokens that represent different gemstones.

Suburbia

 1-4   90 minutes   City building Economic   Card drafting Set collection Tile placement

Players are competing to turn their small town into an efficient and well-functioning urban metropolis. Game play involves a tile placement mechanism, with the hexagonal tiles representing different types of properties and commodities. Your income and reputation will grow as your town does, meaning you will have even more in-game currency to keep developing your city and attract a larger population. The aim is to build an economic engine that will keep bringing in the necessary wealth. The player with the largest population wins.

Sushi Go Party

  2-8 15-20 minutes Food Card drafting
Hand management
Set collection
Simultaneous
action selection

This is a party edition of the bestselling card game *Sushi Go*, which has been adapted for more players. Players are diners at a sushi restaurant and are aiming to create the best combinations and score points. Game play uses a card-drafting mechanism, so each player selects one card that they want to keep, places it face up in front of them and then passes the rest on. The round ends when all the cards have been played, and the game lasts three rounds. The different sushi combinations score different points, and the highest score wins.

Take It Easy

 1-8 20 minutes Abstract Puzzle
Tile placement

Each player has their own hexagonal board and is pursuing their own strategy, but they are all following the same instructions. One player is designated the caller, who selects tiles randomly and tells the others what they are. Each of the hexagonal tiles features three numbered lines, running in different directions. The aim is to place the tiles on the board so all the numbers line up. This is a bit confusing to explain but seems a lot more straightforward when you are looking at the pieces. Play continues until the boards are filled. The numbers on the tiles are multiplied by the number of tiles on the line to give the score. Highest score wins.

Takenoko

 2–4   45 minutes   Animals
Farming  Set collection
Tile placement

Players are members of the Japanese imperial court, who have been entrusted by the emperor to care for a very special panda and tend to the bamboo gardens that feed the animal. The aim is to grow the most bamboo and feed the panda's appetite. The gardens are made up of different hexagonal tiles, and the game is played with cards, counters and little models of the bamboo shoots, the panda and the gardener. Players have to complete their individual objectives – decreed to them via the objective cards – to win the game.

Telestrations

 4–8   30 minutes   Humour
Party game   Drawing
Real-time

This is a simple game of drawing and guessing. Players begin by each drawing something to represent the word they have been given. When the timer runs out, they pass their drawing on, and the next person guesses what it is. They write their guess down and pass it on. The next person looks at the guess but not the drawing, and then draws their own interpretation of the guess, and so on until the work is back with the original drawer. The game comes with dry-wipe notebooks to record the drawings and guesses, and keep them secret on each turn. Players award points to each other for the best drawings and guesses, and they get a point if the final guess is the same as their original word. Highest score wins.

Terraforming Mars

 1-5   120 minutes   Economic
Environmental
Industry/
manufacturing
Science fiction   Card drafting
Hand
management
Tile placement

In the not too distant future, giant corporations are plotting to make Mars habitable for humans. Players take on the role of these corporations and compete to earn victory points. It's quite a complex strategy game that uses several different game mechanics, but that keeps the game interesting as it is possible for fortunes to change quickly.

The Fox in the Forest

 2   30 minutes   Animals
Fantasy   Hand
management
Trick-taking

Game play is similar to trick-taking card games like Whist, in that players must follow suit and can use trump cards; however, it is played using beautifully illustrated cards featuring different fairy tale woodland characters. Players gain points based on how many tricks they have won, but if they are too greedy, they might end up losing.

The Mind

 2-4   15 minutes    Abstract   Co-operative play
Hand
management

This is a game of subtle cues, reading body language and blind luck. Players are working together to beat the game, but they aren't allowed to speak. The cards are numbered 1-100 and the aim is to play each hand onto a discard pile in ascending order. Sounds easy, except you don't know what is in everyone else's hand, so you have to hope you're playing the lowest card to start. The aim is to make it through as many levels as you can, and you have a number of cards equal to the level you are on. Complete 12 levels to win.

The Resistance

 5-10 30 minutes Spies/secret agents Bluffing
Deduction
Partnerships
Simultaneous
action selection

In a dystopian future, players are a group of resistance fighters who are pitted against an oppressive regime. However, there is a spy in the ranks. Players have to deduce who they can trust as they try to carry out their missions.

Ticket to Ride

 2-5 30-60 minutes Trains Card drafting
Hand management
Route/network building
Set collection

Players are pioneering transport magnates who are competing over railway routes. The original game was played on a map of North America, but there is now a series of different spin-offs featuring different geographical regions. It is played using cards and model train cars, which players place on the routes to lay claim to them. Points are scored based on the length of the routes that the players create, and for fulfilling the objectives that are set out on the destination tickets. Highest score wins.

Tip Over

 1 As long as you want Abstract Puzzle

A one-player 3D logic puzzle which will test your sequential reasoning skills, the aim is to create a path by tipping over crates, so that the red tipper man can get to the red crate. There are different challenge cards which show you how to set up the plastic components on the board, and these get progressively more difficult.

Tokyo Highway

 2 30-50 minutes Transport Dexterity
Route/network
building

Players compete to build roadways using the components that come with the game - designs can be as ambitious as you like: the aim is to build bridges over your opponent's roads and roads under your opponent's bridges. When you cross an opponent's road, you get to place a car on that section. The first player to place ten cars wins.

Trivial Pursuit

 2-6 90 minutes Trivia Roll and move
Set collection

Surely this game is such a classic as to need no introduction? Players compete to travel around the board, answering questions to win segments of 'cheese' to go into their plastic wheel tokens. The first to collect all six pieces and answer a final question correctly wins.

Two Rooms and a Boom

 6-30 15 minutes Spies/secret agents Acting
Bluffing
Deduction
Partnerships

A social party game which relies heavily on deduction and trust, players are divided into two teams and must work out who among them is the president (on the blue team) and who is the bomber (on the red team). Everyone is given a character card, but these aren't revealed until later. Players are separated into two different rooms but must try to figure out who is who. They negotiate and exchange hostages. If the bomber is in the same room as the president at the end, the blue team loses.

Viticulture

 1-6   45-90 minutes   Economic Farming   Hand management Worker placement

Players are managers of meagre vineyards in pre-industrial Tuscany and are competing to make their winery the most successful in the region. Move workers around the board and set them to essential tasks to ensure that you can achieve your goal: how you manage them could determine the success of your game.

Welcome to ...

 1-99   25 minutes   City building   Roll and write

Players are architects in 1950s America. The game is played on individual boards and each player is striving to create the best development possible with the cards they have at their disposal. Individual strategy will determine success.

Wits and Wagers

 3-7   25 minutes   Party game Trivia   Betting and wagering Bluffing

This relatively simple game combines trivia and betting, and can be a fun introduction to quiz-based games for those who aren't fans of trivia. The answers to all the questions are numerical, and the players each write a number down and place it on the betting mat. If they are confident that their answer is closest, they bet on it. If they think someone else's is more likely, they back that answer. The player who's won the most after seven questions is the winner.

Yahtzee

 2-10 30 minutes Abstract Roll and write
Press your luck
Set collection

Players take it in turns to roll five dice, and they can roll them up to three times to try to get the best outcome. The numbers, and number combinations, that come up are awarded a score. Players keep track using the scorecards that come with the game (although if you've run out, there are plenty of images online that you could copy – or ideally laminate your own). Scores are tallied and compared at the end.

Zombie Dice

 2-99 10-20 minutes Horror
Zombies  Dice rolling
Press your luck

Players are hungry zombies who want brains but need to avoid getting taken out with a shotgun. The faces on the custom dice represent the victims: on each roll you could win a brain, but you also risk getting shot, ending your turn and losing any brains you've already won. The first to push their luck and win 13 brains wins the game.

REFERENCES AND FURTHER READING

Action for Children (2016). 'Unplugging' from technology (6 January). Available at: https://www.actionforchildren.org.uk/news-and-blogs/whats-new/2016/january/unplugging-from-technology/.

Bell, Robbie and Michael Cornelius (1988). *Board Games Round the World: A Resource Book for Mathematical Investigations* (Cambridge: Cambridge University Press).

Boycott-Owen, Mason (2018). After books and vinyl, board games make a comeback, *The Observer* (13 May). Available at: https://www.theguardian.com/lifeandstyle/2018/may/12/millennials-drive-board-games-revival.

Brown, Stuart (2018). 'Stuart Brown: play is more than fun', *TED.com* [video] (12 March). Available at: https://www.youtube.com/watch?v=HHwXlcHcTHc.

Bush, Nikki (2017). Parenting tips: why rituals are important in family life, *Nikki Bush* [blog] (19 September). Available at: https://nikkibush.com/rituals-are-important-in-family-life/.

Bush, Nikki and Graeme Codrington (2008). *Future-Proof Your Child: Parenting the Wired Generation* (London: Penguin).

Chassapakis, Dimitris (2017). *Journal 29: Interactive Book Game* (n.p.: Primedia eLaunch LLC).

Chow, Scott (2019). How to start a blog in 2019, *The Blog Starter* [blog] (10 May). Available at: https://www.theblogstarter.com/.

Corless, Damian (2010). Teaching life skills using board games? It's child's play … *Independent.ie* (1 November). Available at: https://www.independent.ie/life/family/learning/teaching-life-skills-using-board-games-its-childs-play--26790410.html.

Dewar, Gwen (n.d.). Board games for kids: can they teach critical thinking? *Parenting Science* [blog]. Available at: https://www.parentingscience.com/board-games-for-kids.html.

Dix, Ellie (2019). How to play Rummy, *The Dark Imp* [blog] (27 February). Available at: http://www.thedarkimp.com/games-puzzles/how-to-play-rummy/.

Dix, Ellie (2019). How to play Spaces patience, *The Dark Imp* [blog] (27 February). Available at: http://www.thedarkimp.com/games-puzzles/spaces-patience/.

Dix, Ellie (2019). Stations, *The Dark Imp* [blog] (11 March). Available at: https://www.thedarkimp.com/blog/2019/03/11/stations/.

Dix, Ellie (2019). Tournament organiser, *The Dark Imp* [blog] (9 March). Available at: https://www.thedarkimp.com/blog/2019/03/08/tournament-organiser.

Dix, Paul (2017). *When the Adults Change, Everything Changes: Seismic Shifts in School Behaviour* (Carmarthen: Independent Thinking Press).

Fetell Lee, Ingrid (2018). *Joyful: The Surprising Power of Ordinary Things to Create Extraordinary Happiness* (London: Rider Books).

Graham, Richard (2016). A cure for the fear of missing out? *Huff Post* [blog] (22 May). Available at: https://www.huffingtonpost.co.uk/dr-richard-graham/fear-of-missing-out_b_7349230.

Greenfield, Patrick (2018). Kirstie Allsopp defends decision to smash her children's iPads, *The Guardian* (15 September). Available at: https://www.theguardian.com/tv-and-radio/2018/sep/15/kirstie-allsopp-defends-decision-smash-childrens-ipads.

Health Fitness Revolution (2015). Top 10 health benefits of board games, *Health Fitness Revolution* [blog] (15 May). Available at: http://www.healthfitnessrevolution.com/top-10-health-benefits-board-games/.

Janis-Norton, Noël (2016). *Calmer Easier Happier Screen Time* (London: Yellow Kite).

Knizia, Reiner (2010). *Dice Games Properly Explained* (Blue Terrier Press).

Leana, John, Sam Illingworth and Paul Wake (2018). Unhappy families: using tabletop games as a technology to understand play in education, *Research in Learning Technology*, 26. Available at: https://journal.alt.ac.uk/index.php/rlt/article/view/2027.

Lee, Shen-Li (2017). How to help children develop spatial reasoning skills, *Figur8* [blog] (8 February). Available at: https://www.figur8.net/2017/02/08/developing-spatial-reasoning-skills/.

Mackey, Allyson P., Susanna S. Hill, Susan I. Stone and Silvia A. Bunge (2011). Differential effects of reasoning and speed training in children, *Developmental Science*, 14(3): 582–590.

Parlett, David (1980). *The Penguin Book of Patience* (London: Penguin).

Parlett, David (2008). *The Penguin Book of Card Games* (London: Penguin).

Pennant, Jennie and Liz Woodham (2013). Developing logical thinking: the place of strategy games, *NRICH Maths* (November). Available at: https://nrich.maths.org/10019.

Price, Catherine (2018). *How to Break Up with Your Phone: The 30-Day Plan to Take Back Your Life* (London: Trapeze).

Rhodes, Jean (2015). 10 reasons mentors should play cards with their mentees, *The Chronicle of Evidence-Based Mentoring* [blog] (12 April). Available at: https://www.evidencebasedmentoring.org/play-cards/.

Robinson, Lawrence, Melinda Smith and Jeanne Segal (2018). Laughter is the best medicine, *Help Guide* [blog] (November). Available at: https://www.helpguide.org/articles/mental-health/laughter-is-the-best-medicine.htm.

Robinson, Lawrence, Melinda Smith, Jeanne Segal and Jennifer Shubin (2018). The benefits of play for adults, *Help Guide* [blog] (November). Available at: https://www.helpguide.org/articles/mental-health/benefits-of-play-for-adults.htm.

Sackson, Sid (2011). *A Gamut of Games* (New York: Dover Press).

Sinek, Simon (2018). The infinite game [video], *The New York Times Conferences* (31 May). Available at: https://www.youtube.com/watch?v=tye525dkfi8.

Sinek, Simon (2019). *The Infinite Game: How Great Businesses Achieve Long-Lasting Success* (London: Portfolio Penguin).

Telegraph, The (2018). NHS to treat child gaming addicts as young as 12 isolated from friends (31 July). Available at: https://www.telegraph.co.uk/news/2018/07/31/nhs-treat-child-gaming-addicts-young-12-isolated-friends/.

Verstraeten, Julie (2019). The rise of board games, *Medium* (21 April). Available at: https://medium.com/@Juliev/the-rise-of-board-games-a7074525a3ec.

Viggiano, Alessandro, Emanuela Viggiano, Anna Di Costanzo, Andrea Viggiano, Eleonora Andreozzi, Vincenzo Romano, Ines Rianna, et al. (2015). Kaledo, a board game for nutrition education of children and adolescents at school: cluster randomized controlled trial of healthy lifestyle promotion, *European Journal of Pediatrics*, 174(2): 217–228.

Wallace, Kelly (2016). Half of teens think they're addicted to their smartphones, *CNN* (29 July). Available at: https://edition.cnn.com/2016/05/03/health/teens-cell-phone-addiction-parents/index.html.

WEBSITES

For reviews of family-friendly games, visit: https://www.theboardgamefamily.com/. (This is an independent site which is in no way affiliated with this book.)

The online bible of board gaming can be found at: https://boardgamegeek.com/.

A publisher of free and cheap games is: https://cheapass.com/.

For board game reviews and top ten lists, visit: https://www.dicetower.com/.

Find your local board game store: http://findyourgamestore.co.uk/.

For more resources, blogs and services from Ellie Dix, visit: https://www.thedarkimp.com.

ABOUT THE AUTHOR

A teacher and educationalist, and former co-owner and director of Pivotal Education, Ellie Dix has been obsessed with board games from an early age. Ellie firmly believes that board games have positively influenced her ability to solve problems, manage failure and experiment with multiple paths to success - and she now puts her teaching skills, understanding of behaviour and experience with gamification to use by helping parents to introduce board games to family life.

@EllieDixTweets

www.thedarkimp.com